HOW DOES THIS WORKOUT DIFFER FROM ALL OTHER FITNESS PROGRAMS? BETTY WEIDER TELLS YOU HOW . . .

"There are literally thousands of fitness plans on the market. But most of them require spending over an hour a day working out, and that you go to a fitness center to do so. With this program, you can work at home—thirty minutes per session, with a minimum of equipment—a few sets of dumbbells (hand-held weights) and a bench. If you don't want to invest in a bench, you can even do the few exercises that require one at the edge of a bed or sofa!

"But what's more important about this program as opposed to other programs is, it works. As the wife of Joe Weider, the father of bodybuilding principles, and as co-founder and writer for *Shape* magazine, I have learned exactly what it takes to get in shape in record time—and I've decided to share these secrets with you.

"There's no need for lifting heavy weights or spending hours in a gym. If you want to reshape your body, all you need is to use free weights the right way! It's as simple as that."

BETTER AND BETTER

Six Weeks to a Great Shape at Any Age!

BETTY WEIDER

and

JOYCE L. VEDRAL, Ph.D.

A DELL TRADE PAPERBACK

A DELL TRADE PAPERBACK

Published by
Dell Publishing
a division of
Bantam Doubleday Dell Publishing Group, Inc.
666 Fifth Avenue
New York, New York 10103

It is essential before undertaking any workout program that you consult your physician to ascertain whether any forms of physical exertion may be harmful to you. Your physician's recommendations should always be followed.

CREDITS

Cover, back cover, and exercise photographs by Harry Langdon
Cover design by Robert Santora
Book design by Stanley S. Drate/Folio Graphics Co., Inc.
Joyce Vedral's exercise leotard by (`kȯ-fē) of California
Betty Weider's exercise leotard—a Gilda Marx Breathables Flexatard
Betty Weider's cover leotard by Carushka, Van Nuys, California
Hair and makeup by Stephen Reiley
Clothing Stylist and Coordinator—Meg Freeman
Photography Direction—James Camperos

ISBN: 0-440-50313-2

Printed in the United States of America

Published simultaneously in Canada

February 1993

10 9 8 7 6 5 4 3 2 1

CWO

DEDICATION

To the women who read my columns in *Shape* and *Muscle and Fitness* magazines and who have asked me to write a book that will help get them in shape once and for all!

ACKNOWLEDGMENTS

To Jill Lamar and Trish Todd, our astute and sensitive editors, for your careful attention to this project.

To Leslie Schnur, for your insight in realizing that the time is right!

To family and friends, for your continual love and support.

To Rick Balkin, agent for this book, for your relentless attention to this project.

To Laurie Einstein Koszuta, for your help with the medical research and for going the extra mile.

Contents

Introduction

We've all heard the expression, "You're not getting older, you're getting better." But the simple truth is, we're all—even a twenty-one-year-old beauty—getting older, but we're not all getting better . . . unless! Unless what? Unless we do exactly what needs to be done to ensure that our bodies improve rather than decline with age. The purpose of this book is to show you how to reverse the tide—to add beautiful, perfectly shaped "mini" muscles to your body so that you look and feel younger as time goes by.

I am now in my mid fifties, and my coauthor, Joyce Vedral, is in her late forties. Yet the two of us have been able to regain and retain our youthful appearance by working out with light weights for a mere thirty minutes a few times a week. You can do the same—and by the way, you can certainly use this book if you are a "youngster" of thirty or forty! (Yes, twenty-year-olds can use it too!)

When a woman reaches her forties she actually has an advantage over younger women. She is more mature and has gained wisdom and knowledge. Maturity has taught her not to expect instant results. Wisdom has shown her that with time, consistent, intelligent effort brings inevitable results. Knowledge has made it clear to her that when she wishes to achieve a result most effectively, she must go to professionals—experts in the field—people with a track record. And calmness has taught her to look at the facts.

After thirty the average woman loses a half pound of muscle a year. If something isn't done to replace this muscle loss, in time she becomes softer and softer and her metabolism slows down more and more, until she is made of soft, unshapely fat rather than firm, shapely muscle. An older woman realizes that even if she weighs the same as she did when she was twenty-one, unless she begins to work out the right way (as described in this book), her body composition will change for the worse. But she doesn't panic when she faces these facts. She does something about it.

If you've picked up this book after having failed at other fitness programs, perhaps for the first time in your life you've come to the right place. Why? Because I am not sixteen. I do not propose miracle cures. I have been around long enough to know that changing a body takes time—but, joyfully, not nearly as much time as it would take if you went to a health spa, randomly picked up weights, and hoped to "get lucky." I have been advising women on fitness in my columns in *Shape* and *Muscle and Fitness* for over three decades and have had the pleasure of guiding countless seemingly "hopeless cases" to success. Joyce Vedral has spent many an hour instructing women on how to get in shape and answering call-in questions on national and local television and radio shows.

Together we've realized that what women want today is not an unrealistic, quick cure-all, and not a grueling, time-consuming routine, but a moderate yet effective program that will reshape the body in the minimum amount of time with the most efficient use of energy.

Not so long ago, once a woman approached her late twenties she already began to see herself as going "over the hill." These days, with all the medical and psychological knowledge available, women in their forties, fifties, and even older can remain vibrant and appealing because they have a greater degree of physical fitness and vitality than ever before. In fact, studies have shown that even people in their nineties can make significant gains in muscle tone and strength with resistance training. So you see, there's no excuse for any of us. We can start at any age and reap the benefits.

I'll never forget a conversation I had with Sylvester Stallone. When I asked him what was most instrumental in shaping his amazing career, he surprised me by saying that it was an exercise program. He told me that at an early age he got hold of the bodybuilding magazine *Muscle and Fitness* (published by my husband, Joe Weider), and began working out. He said that it was the continual discipline he had to exert in overcoming his moods, circumstances, and other obstacles that later enabled him to become successful in writing, acting, and producing. The building of his body, as it turned out, netted Sylvester Stallone a lot more than a strong, healthy body.

His story didn't surprise me. Many studies have demonstrated that physically fit people are more intellectually inclined and emotionally stable than those who are not physically fit. In fact, there are studies indicating that a large percentage of college dropouts are significantly less fit than those who remain in school, graduate, and go on to successful careers. There is indeed something about physical exercise that translates into mental discipline.

BETTER
AND
BETTER

1 Better and Better

It doesn't matter what age you are. Whether you're fifteen or fifty, exercise is for you. If you begin a disciplined program now, you'll see results. If you are younger, great. You have a head start. If you are older and have not exercised much previously, you have a unique advantage. Since you have never stimulated your muscles in a systematic, appropriate way before, for the first time in your life you will see your body beginning to be reshaped into its perfect form. You'll watch your shape change before your very eyes—and in only a matter of weeks.

The Program

You won't have to devote every waking moment to exercise, and you won't suffer hunger pangs as the result of a severe diet. The only requirement is a firm commitment of *thirty minutes every other day*. You'll be working with light weights, and you will not get big, bulky muscles—rather, you will become firm, shapely, strong, and toned. On alternate days you will be encouraged to engage in an aerobic or sports activity of your choice.

After six weeks your body will be firmer, stronger, healthier, and more energetic, and in addition, significantly reshaped. The result of your consistent, deliberate effort will be clearly demonstrated in the mirror—a living trophy to celebrate your victory.

What's more, you'll feel better. You'll have developed muscles to help support your joints—muscles that will act as shock absorbers so that you'll no longer walk around with mysterious aches and pains. In addition, you'll be able to eat more food than before without getting fat, because the development of small, shapely muscles will have sped up your metabolism. In fact, even while sleeping you'll burn more calories, because well-conditioned muscles use up about twenty-five percent of your caloric expenditure while you sleep. In short, in six weeks you'll look, feel, and be the better for your alternate-day half hour investment.

Why Does This Program Work?

This regimen succeeds where others fail because it's based upon the time-tested body-shaping principles of the trainer of champions, my husband, Joe Weider. A beautiful body is not merely a matter of good luck or good genetics. It's a matter of correct and consistent training.

What causes this workout to be effective where other popular workouts fail? Why is it that this workout guarantees a reshaped body in just months, where other workouts promise only the burning of some calories and slight muscle stimulation?

The Key Principles of This Workout

The two most important principles of this workout are: *the split routine* and *muscle isolation*. These two principles distinguish the Weider system of training from many other systems—including the most popular on the market.

The Split Routine

The split routine involves splitting up your workout into parts. Rather than working the entire body (all nine body parts) in one day, you'll exercise one group of body parts on a given day, another group the next, and so on. For the purpose of this workout, you'll be splitting your routine in two. That is, you will be exercising five body parts on one workout day and the other four body parts on the next workout day. This convenient two-day split fits neatly into the alternate-day workout plan.

For those who have the luxury of working out six days a week, a three-day split is also possible. However, such workouts are typical of competitive bodybuilders rather than those who work out to stay in shape and achieve muscle tone and shape.

The reason for the split routine is twofold. First, it is virtually impossible to give your maximum effort to a workout if you attempt to exercise your entire body in one session.

If you try to cover all nine body parts on one workout day, chances are, by the time you get to your sixth body part, you'll begin to experience fatigue and even boredom. Not only will you neglect to give the exercises your best effort (maximum strength and strict form), but you may become resentful of the amount of work you're being forced to do and literally "throw in the towel." It's a much better idea to exercise no more than five body parts in any given workout session.

Second, in order to achieve optimum growth and development, muscles need at least forty-eight hours to completely recuperate from a workout before restimulation. Since you'll be resting every other day, your muscles will automatically get that needed forty-eight-hour rest. However, doing a split routine will allow you to "work ahead" or catch up, by working out two, three, or even four days in a row (as discussed in Chapter 4). So in the case of this workout, the split routine serves not only as insurance that you'll give the workout your best shot, but also that you'll have the opportunity to work out two days in a row without sacrificing optimum muscle growth and development.

Muscle Isolation

Did you ever notice that some people who work out in health spas jump around from machine to machine, exercising one body part and then another with no particular plan in mind? Perhaps they do one shoulder exercise, then a chest exercise, and then an abdominal exercise. Why do they proceed in this manner? It may be because their shoulders are tired after one exercise, so they think it's a good idea to give that area a rest. It may be that the shoulder machine they wanted to use next was occupied, so they figured it would be a good idea to use any available machine.

Unfortunately, you cannot just do what is convenient or comfortable when working out. In order to be challenged to the point of growth and development, a muscle must be exercised to its capacity or near capacity. In essence, this means that you should perform all of the exercises for one body part before advancing to the next. It's not enough to tease the muscle with only one exercise and then move on to another muscle and tease it. Even if you eventually return to the original body part with a second exercise, you have lost the intensity effect. The muscle has had too long to rest, and it will not grow to capacity. The end result is the burning of some calories with little or no change in body shape.

(The body is shaped by the muscles attached to the bones. It is only by reshaping and firming the muscles that the body becomes tight and toned.)

How Much Time Will You Have to Spend Working Out?

Your total time investment will be thirty minutes every other day—with an optimal additional twenty to thirty minutes of walking or low-impact aerobics on the alternate days. That's it. You'll find out exactly what you have to do in Chapter 3.

How Does This Workout Differ from Other Fitness Programs?

There are literally thousands of fitness plans on the market. But most of them require spending more than an hour a day working out and going to a fitness center to do so. With this program you can work at home—thirty minutes per session, with a minimum of equipment: a few sets of dumbbells (hand-held weights) and a bench. If you don't want to invest in a bench, you can even do the few exercises that require one at the edge of a bed or sofa!

But what's more important about this program as opposed to other programs is, it works. As the wife of Joe Weider, the father of bodybuilding principles, and as cofounder and writer for *Shape* magazine, I have learned exactly what it takes to get in shape in record time—and I've decided to share those secrets with you.

There's no need for lifting heavy weights or spending hours in a gym. If you want to reshape your body, all you need to do is use free weights the right way! It's as simple as that.

How Long Will It Take to See Results?

You'll begin to see and feel results almost immediately. In a week you'll sense a new energy. In two weeks your walking and sitting posture will improve. In three weeks you'll begin to notice a difference in muscle tone. In four, you'll start to see a change in the shape of certain muscles. In six weeks you'll see major changes in all of your muscles. Your stubborn body parts, such as your abdominal area, your buttocks, and your thighs, may take longer. In a year's time, if you work hard and follow the program, you should reach near perfection for your body. However, as you continue to work out you'll see subtle improvement as time goes by. It will indeed be true that you won't merely be getting older (every living person is, you know), you'll be getting better.

It may take six months to achieve major changes in those stubborn hip, buttock, and thigh areas. If you're more than eight pounds overweight, your abdominal development won't be apparent until you lose the excess body fat around your stomach.

In addition, each person has certain body parts that seem to leap to progress and others that lag behind. Your back may take forever to develop, while your shoulders may respond immediately. Your triceps may lag behind, while your biceps may show immediate improvement. For another woman the reverse may be true. But no matter what, we promise you, if you stick to this program, no matter how stubborn your particular body part is, you will see dramatic results in six months at the most, and near perfection in a year—*if* you stick to the program.

Your progress will also depend upon your age. Naturally, a twenty-five-year-old will progress a little faster than a fifty-five-year-old. There are, however, some twenty-five-year-olds whose genetics cause them to progress at the same rate as a forty-five-year-old, and some forty-five-year-olds who can progress as a twenty-five-year-old would. In any case, no matter what your age or your genetics, if you stick to the program, in time you will see major progress.

Exercise Creates Vitality—Both Mental and Physical

When people ask me why I exercise, they're often surprised by my answer. Perhaps they expect me to say the obvious: "To keep in shape." But to be honest, that's not my main reason for exercising, although I couldn't imagine not having the shaping and toning effect of exercise.

My main reason for exercising is the physical and mental fitness it gives me. It makes me feel strong, energetic, and healthy. It gives me vitality and helps me fight depression.

Exercise sets off a chain reaction. You exercise—and your body becomes stronger. You begin to feel healthier and more energetic. This puts you in a better mood. Your elevated mood causes your immune system to strengthen so that you're better able to ward off illnesses that might otherwise penetrate your body. Your improved mood and good health cause you to gain a new, confident outlook on life. You begin to take chances and challenges you were previously reluctant to attempt. In short, the quality of your life improves in every way imaginable.

Mental Benefits

Stress Relief

The exercises prescribed in this book have been proven to significantly relieve stress. When you work out with weights or perform an aerobic activity, and when you utilize a minimum of fifty percent of your maximum oxygen supply for twenty or more minutes, you reduce your blood pressure and heart rate.

Here's how it works. When you experience stress, the adrenal medulla in the adrenal glands releases the catecholamines epinephrine (also known as adrenaline) and norepinephrine. When this happens you're in a "fight or flight mode." Your heart beats faster, your metabolism rises, and you're generally anxious. Your blood volume increases and flows through your muscles, brain, and heart at a rapid rate—and your blood pressure is raised.

What causes this kind of stress? A personal relationship that means a lot to you—and isn't going well—is a prime agitator. Another one is overwork and general mental fatigue. A third might be a threat of any kind—loss of your job, the death of a loved one, a personal illness, and so on.

Once stress occurs, your blood pressure rises, causing pathophysiological changes including increased levels of free fatty acids and serum cholesterol due to sympathetic activation of the liver. Increased platelet adhesion and aggregation in the arteries can occur because of elevated circulating epinephrine and norepinephrine. If the stress is emotional, sometimes the sodium level will also rise, and fluid retention occurs. In addition, potassium is lost because of the increase in epinephrine. The cumulative effect of all the above can lead to a serious threat to the heart.

Now for the good news. Researchers have discovered that any exercise that can raise your heart level to fifty percent of maximum or more can reduce the levels of epinephrine and norepinephrine and thus reduce your blood pressure and heart rate. The most wonderful thing about this discovery is that exercise shortens the amount of time it takes for a stressed person's blood pressure and heart rate to return to normal. This reduced time helps decrease the possibility of heart attack.

Mood Elevation

After using the thirty-minute workout for about ten minutes, you'll experience a mood elevation—a kind of euphoria. This "natural high" is caused by the release of endorphins, an opiate-like enzyme that produces a relaxed, euphoric feeling.

The endorphins released act on specific receptor sites in the brain. After intense exercise (you must work at least fifty percent of your maximum capacity—as you will be during the thirty-minute workout and the optional aerobic and sports activities) the opiates in the bloodstream and the brain are five times higher than they are during rest periods.

The opiates in the brain and bloodstream account for the natural high produced by exercise, a high that lasts from fifteen to sixty minutes. Small wonder many people come back again and again to exercise! Whether on a conscious or subconscious level, they're looking for that wonderful relief of tension, that natural high—the one they got the last time they worked out, the one that carries with it no detrimental consequences but rather positive results above and beyond the high itself (a shapely body, a sound heart and lungs, improved posture, stronger bones, and on and on).

Increased Self-Confidence

There's a definite carryover from physical to mental fitness. If you can get your body in shape, your mind quickly follows suit. In fact, psychologists and medical doctors agree that exercise is even more effective than dieting to increase self-esteem and self-image, which carries over into every aspect of life.

Added Self-Discipline

Once you've established a routine of working out and are true to your commitment, you'll find that the self-discipline you've established in the area of fitness will spill over into other areas of your life. When you don't feel like completing a certain household chore, you'll find yourself doing it anyway, just because it has to be done. When you're not in the mood to make a certain important phone call, you'll find yourself gathering your forces and making the call anyway. When the thought of dealing with a certain business client tempts you to run in the other direction, you will harness your energy and take care of the business at hand. In short, this newly established discipline can help you have a more productive, fulfilling life.

Physical Benefits of Exercise

A Firm, Fit Body

Your entire body, not just your abdominal area, buttocks, and thighs, will be tight, toned, and well-shaped. Nothing will "jiggle." Your clothing will look better on you. But more important, you'll no longer feel the need to hide your body when in the nude or in a bathing suit. Perhaps for the first time in your life you will seek, rather than avoid, opportunities to display your bare back and arms, thighs, hips, and stomach.

Increased Strength

Nothing makes a woman feel older than not being able to do something physically that she could previously do with no great effort. Conversely, nothing makes a woman feel younger than being able to do something physically—with ease—that was previously difficult, or impossible.

After following this program for a few months you'll experience a delightful increase in strength. For example, even though you're probably not overly concerned with the look of your biceps muscles (most women are too busy worrying about their buttocks, thighs, and abdominals), you'll find that after working out for a few months you'll be able to take care of daily business with much more ease than before. For example, simple household chores, such as carrying a garbage can to the curb, washing windows, pulling and pushing a vacuum cleaner, picking up a bucket of water with one hand (a gallon of water weighs eight pounds), painting a wall or ceiling, or lifting a heavy object, will become comparatively easy. The feeling you'll experience is one of power and energy when you find yourself sailing through chores that were at one time enervating.

This happens because your biceps muscles, along with your other eight muscle groups (triceps, chest, shoulders, back, abdominals, calves, thighs, and buttocks), will be stronger and will no longer tire as readily as they did when they were weaker.

Increased Metabolism—Eat More Without Getting Fat

Vigorous exercise also speeds up your metabolism for hours after you've stopped working out. In other words, you continue to burn more calories per minute long after you have ceased exercising.

You may have wondered why men usually can eat more than women without getting fat. The simple answer is muscle. Pound for pound, men tend to have a higher body composition of muscle than women.

In addition, muscle is the only body tissue that's metabolically active (that is, it burns energy even when at rest), while skin, bones, fat, blood, and other body materials are inactive. In essence, the more muscle weight you have on your body, the more you'll be able to eat without getting fat.

How is this possible? Why does increased muscle mass raise metabolism? The cells enlarge when fibers in the muscle thicken and increase in number. The muscle then uses more energy to sustain its larger size. In fact, when enlarged muscles are tested, specific nutrients show gains within the enlarged fibers. More simply, the larger the muscle, the more calories consumed to maintain that muscle.

Decreased Appetite

Exercise not only burns calories and helps reshape your body. It also helps decrease your appetite by stabilizing insulin and blood sugar. In addition, exercise helps you feel satisfied more quickly when you eat, because it stimulates the production of hormones that raise your blood-fat level. The resulting fatty acids circulating in your bloodstream cause the feeling of "fullness."

Weight Loss in Body Fat

Weight gain and loss is usually a result of adding or subtracting fat from the body. In simple terms, weight is gained whenever there is an imbalance between the amount of calories consumed and used. That is, when a woman eats more than her body can immediately use, the excess calories are converted into fat and stored for future use.

The opposite is true for weight loss. When a woman has a greater energy output than the number of calories consumed, weight is lost, because there are no excess calories left to store. This simple principle is called "negative energy balance" (energy expenditure exceeds intake).

As you do the thirty-minute alternate-day workout, you'll burn two hundred to three hundred calories each time you exercise, depending upon how intensely you work out. For each twelve days that you do the thirty-minute workout, you'll lose a pound of fat. (It takes a calorie deficit of 3,500 calories to lose a pound of fat.)

Strong, Healthy Bones

It has recently been discovered that working with weights not only slows down the loss of bone as a woman ages, but in fact increases bone density.

A recent study done with regularly exercising postmenopausal women at McMaster University showed that the women had increased the bone mass in their spine by nine percent. (The same women also increased their muscle strength and size by twenty percent.)

Most women reach their peak bone mass at the age of thirty-five. They begin to lose about one percent of bone a year after that, and postmenopausal women can lose as much as six percent of their bone mass during the first five years after the start of change of life. It's crucial that women begin an aggressive program of diet and exercise not only to stave off bone loss but to increase bone density. The added bonus of having strong, healthy bones is insurance against easy fracture.

The best exercise program is one that includes resistance training working specific skeletal muscles and aerobic activities that are weight bearing (bearing the weight of the body during performance). This is our exercise program! This workout will result in the "youthing" of your bones rather than the aging or deterioration of them.

Improved Posture

Antigravity muscles (located in the back, abdomen, buttocks, front thighs, and calves) help us stand upright. These muscles continually fight the force of gravity, which would otherwise pull our bodies down and cause us to walk on "all fours."

When we're young most of us have no trouble with our posture. We walk upright and with proper body alignment. As time begins to take its toll (after age thirty), we begin to see changes in our sitting, standing, and walking stance. The pelvis begins to tilt forward, the back begins to sway, and the neck begins to thrust forward.

Why does this happen? As mentioned before, every year after thirty, muscles atrophy slightly. In short, they become weaker and less able to do the job of fighting the force of gravity, of keeping our bodies in an upright position with proper alignment. However, if you engage in an appropriate resistance-training program such as the one described in this book, you not only replace the muscle that would otherwise be atrophying, you add additional muscle to your entire body. This added musculature provides the strength and support needed to allow your body to remain erect and with the proper alignment you had in your youth. In fact, I now have much better posture than I had when I was in my twenties!

So even if you've had multiple pregnancies, gained and lost a lot of weight over the years, or have continually worn high-heeled shoes (all contributors to bad posture and improper body alignment), you can improve your posture tremendously by developing your muscles as prescribed in this workout.

Increased Energy and Youth

Even moderate exercise decreases fatigue and increases energy. Increased energy removes the feeling of being run down all the time. In fact, it helps to create the opposite feeling—one of being ready to go all the time.

When you work out properly and keep yourself in shape, you'll not only look and feel up to twenty years younger, you can actually be up to twenty years younger. Think of it this way: You're a fifty-something-year-old in better shape, physically, than a twenty-five-year-old.

The fact is, there's a vast difference between physiological and chronological age, and exercise can make all the difference. By doing our workout and by following the nutritional suggestions, you can indeed have more energy and actually be physiologically younger in every way. When you exercise properly and consistently, you actually set your age regression clock at a higher level.

Reduced Aches and Pains

Since weakened muscles cause posture imbalance, strengthening the muscles will work to recreate the body alignment and in turn relieve the aches and pains of your back, hips, and feet. In addition, the strengthened muscles in the abdominal, hip, and back areas cause great improvement in overall muscular coordination.

When faced with a physical challenge, such as a sudden jarring or jerking motion, a strong, muscular body will be better able to withstand the impact than one with flabby, sagging muscles that force the body to change its mechanics and be thrown off balance. End result: less likelihood of injury and chronic aches and pains.

Youthful Skin

As you exercise, increased blood flow to the skin will provide your skin with oxygen and help improve its color, elasticity, and general health. The aging of your skin will be retarded, and as a result your skin will become more supple and remain tight for a longer period of time than if you had not exercised.

Resistance training will also help keep your skin taut and decrease sagging. This is due to a combination of muscle hypertrophy (growth), which tightens the skin around those muscles, and increased collagen in the skin.

Improved Sports Ability

Whatever your sport, if you're stronger and more flexible, your skill will also improve—and by following this workout you'll be more powerful and agile. In fact, professional sportsmen and -women regularly work out with weights and do aerobic activities with the specific goal of improving their performance in their particular sport.

Lower Blood Pressure and Cardiovascular Benefits

Countless studies have shown that moderate, appropriate exercise helps reduce the risk of cardiovascular disease and lowers blood pressure and cholesterol levels. In addition, exercising as described in this book, especially if you opt to do the alternate-day aerobic workout, will help give you a strong heart and healthy lungs that will operate without a strain at between sixty and eighty-five percent of capacity! No longer will you be out of breath when you climb a flight of stairs!

Easier Menopause

Have we got good news for you! "Change of life," which usually occurs in women between forty-five and fifty-five years old, no longer has to be a dreaded experience. For one thing, you'll no longer have to deal with monthly cramps, mood changes, and cyclic bloating. You can say good-bye to those things forever. Once the menses cease and ovarian hormones are no longer secreted, you don't have to worry about getting pregnant. You can throw your birth control devices out the window, but fortunately not your sex drive, because as you well know, it is alive and well—in fact, more alive than ever.

There's even good news about dealing with the sometimes unpleasant symptoms that accompany menopause. It has recently been proved that an exercise program like ours can significantly raise the level of plasma epinephrine and norepinephrine and reduce muscle tension and anxiety. In fact, our workout program can also reduce insomnia, an annoying problem that plagues many menopausal women.

In addition, if you're in the menopausal stage, this workout and concomitant eating plan (Chapter 5) can help save your life! Because menopause significantly decreases estrogen levels, cholesterol, especially the "bad cholesterol" (LDL), tends to rise. Because of this, women in the postmenopausal period are more susceptible to heart disease. (See Chapter 5 for a full discussion of cholesterol.) However, it has been demonstrated that an exercise program like ours can help to lower your LDL ratios. In short, this program can literally save your life.

Arrested Muscle Atrophy in Older Women

Many women ask us if hormonal changes after thirty, forty, fifty, or older account for muscle atrophy, and they wonder whether or not working out is a waste of time. Although hormones can be blamed for some of the problems women face as they go through menopause, they cannot be blamed for muscle atrophy. Loss of muscle is due to the slight atrophy of muscle every year after thirty *if* a person falls into the rut of becoming more and more inactive. In fact, it has been demonstrated time and again that women (and men alike) can and do increase their muscle mass as they age if they engage in an appropriate resistance-training program.

As far as weight gain is concerned, there is absolutely no evidence that supports the notion that weight gain occurs as a direct result of menopause. In fact, if weight gain does occur, you can be pretty sure that it is the result of inactivity and/or overeating!

The Difference Between Feminine and Masculine Muscularity

Don't worry. This workout will not cause you to develop large, bulky muscles, because you will be using very light weights and will be working out only thirty minutes a session. Professional bodybuilders lift extremely heavy weights and work out in daily two-hour sessions.

Instead of developing bulky muscles, you'll develop small, sensuous curves. In other words, where fat once was, muscle tone will be. You'll feel firm instead of mushy, and you'll be burning extra calories all day long as a side benefit.

In addition, men naturally develop muscles more readily than women. Why? Their bodies produce more than ten times the amount of testosterone (a hormone that stimulates muscular growth) that women's bodies produce.

You may have seen extremely muscular women in magazines or on television. Chances are, these women are professional bodybuilders who spend most of their time working out. Their goal is to become as muscular as possible, so they lift progressively heavier and heavier weights. In the past, some of these women were foolish enough to ingest steroids, which contain the male hormone testosterone, which caused a great and unnatural increase in muscularity. Fortunately, thanks to the efforts of Joe and Ben Weider and the IFBB (International Federation of Bodybuilding), steroid testing is now a regular part of competitive bodybuilding. In time, the ingestion of steroids will be a thing of the past. For our purposes, however, have no fear. You will not look like a man by performing the exercises described in our workout.

Why Not Just Exercise Your "Out of Control" Body Parts and Leave the Rest of Your Body Alone?

Your body posture and overall appearance is greatly affected by the balance of your muscle development. For example, a woman can do hundreds of sit-ups and leg raises, watch her diet, and as a result achieve her goal of a flat stomach. But because she does no back or shoulder exercises, the muscles in those areas will have gradually atrophied, so when she walks her shoulders will be hunched forward and she'll be slightly stooped over. Because she has neglected to exercise her biceps and triceps, her arms will not only appear pencil-thin, giving her the appearance of a frail older woman, but she will have unsightly fat hanging from the back of her upper arm (the triceps). Even if her legs are thin, they will not be shapely. In fact, instead of a firm, sensuous muscle on her thigh, she will have excess skin hanging over her kneecap.

By exercising each body part individually, you can reverse the natural course of the aging process—the atrophy of each muscle (about ten percent a year after age forty). If you do nothing to replace that muscle loss, what will happen to you as you age is apparent. You will literally wither away (unless of course you replace the atrophying muscles with fat, in which case you will become shapeless and weak).

There's no way around it. If you want to look young and feel young, and in fact *be* young, you have to respect all the muscles of your body, not just a select few. Of course, there's no reason why you can't devote a little extra time to some troublesome body parts (as we'll discuss in Chapter 4).

Use Your Mind to Your Greatest Advantage in Helping Reshape Your Body

As you read this book, get a mental picture of how you want to look a year from now. Then, as you follow our diet and exercise plan, continually visualize your body evolving into that image.

Visualization and mental imagery is not new to athletes. The renowned golf champion Jack Nicklaus regularly uses mental imagery. He "sees" the ball falling into the cup before he ever taps it with his golf club. You need to do the same thing. "See" your entire body being transformed into the image you have in mind, before you even move a muscle.

In addition, every time you perform an exercise described in this book, picture the muscle you're working being transformed into the shape you have in mind. "Tell" that body part to get into that shape, and in time it will. Such mental cooperation will help get you to your goal twice as fast as if you hadn't used this method.

How to Think About This Program—and Fitness Work in General

Think about fitness as part of your life—something that you do every day in order to ensure life itself. In other words, think of this fitness program as a life insurance policy, but not just a life insurance policy—a quality-life guarantee. After all, what good is it merely to be alive if you don't feel good enough to enjoy it, or if you're so unhappy with your physical appearance that it diverts your mind to thoughts of shame? Negative self-imagery drains energy that could be used in much more productive ways.

Realize, too, that in the area of fitness a little bit goes a long way. A small amount of consistent effort can actually extend your life. It has recently been demonstrated in a study reported in *The Journal of the American Medical Association* that moderate exercise (such as described in this workout) significantly reduces your chances of dying of cancer, heart disease, and a host of other disorders.

It's No Longer an Option

Our daily ablutions are not optional. We wake up and shower, brush our teeth, and perform other routine hygienic necessities. We must also tend to the physical requirements of our health and fitness program—not just a maintenance program, but an improvement program, so that indeed it can be said that we are not merely getting older day by day, but we are in fact getting better and better. As you read the following chapters you'll find out exactly how to make sure that happens.

Most of us have gone through a stage or two in our lives where we went overboard on something. For some it may have been fanatical dieting—until we were paper-thin. For others it may have been a running kick—or we "aerobicized" ourselves to near extinction. For others it may have been a total commitment to a given sport.

The tendency to overdo is the affliction of youth. Thank goodness, after a certain point the wisdom of time kicks in and one realizes that, indeed, the Bible and other great literature were right: The secret to good health and supreme happiness is balance.

That's the secret of this book. Not too much of this or that—a balance.

2 All You Need to Know

There's no reason to feel threatened when beginning a fitness program—especially if the program is simple, clearly explained, and sticks to the basics.

I've been involved in fitness for many years and have learned to make things simple so that people who know nothing about resistance training, body shaping, or working out in general can quickly pick up the information needed and "go."

In this chapter you'll learn all you need to know to get started. You'll become familiar with the basic principles of body shaping and the Weider principles that have been used by champion bodybuilders since their invention by Joe Weider over fifty years ago—the principles used not only by champion female bodybuilders such as Rachel McLish and Cory Everson, but by many celebrities as well.

Workout Vocabulary

During the course of your workout you'll encounter the following words. To make your exercise life simple, I have provided a brief definition of each term. For your learning convenience the terms are described in order of expanding usage. For example, once you know what an exercise is, you'll learn that you must do "repetitions"; a group of movements that comprise a "set." After you do a set, you will "rest," and so on.

Exercise. The particular body-shaping movement being performed. For example, the leg raise is an abdominal *exercise.*

Repetition or rep. The complete movement of a given exercise, from starting point to midpoint and back to starting point again. For example, one *repetition* of the leg raise involves raising the legs off the floor until they are perpendicular to the floor (midpoint) and then returning them to the floor (starting point).

Set. A specified number of repetitions to be performed without resting. For example, in this workout one *set* will be fifteen repetitions of the leg raise before taking a rest.

Rest. A brief pause between sets. The purpose of the rest is to allow the working muscle time to recuperate. For example, in this workout you'll *rest* about thirty seconds between sets.

Routine. All of the exercises performed for a given body part. For example, in this workout your abdominal *routine* consists of the crunch, the knee-up, the floor side-bend, and the sit-up with a twist.

Workout. The combination of all exercises done on a given day. For example, in this program your hips/buttocks *workout* day two consists of the following routines: thighs, buttocks, back, and biceps.

The next group of definitions involves muscle contraction and extension, pressure on the muscle, and muscle appearance as a result of the work.

Flex. To contract the muscle by shortening it. For example, when performing the biceps curl, the biceps is contracted when you bend your arm to its highest point. At this juncture your biceps muscle "bulges." When we say flex the muscle as hard as possible, we mean consciously squeeze or contract the muscle as intensely as you can, over and above the normal bending or flexing position.

Stretch. To elongate a relaxed muscle. For example, the biceps muscle is stretched when you bring your arm down to its lowest position. At this point your biceps muscle seems to flatten out. When we say "feel the stretch" in the muscle, we mean cooperate with the elongating muscle by stretching it just a little farther. A stretch is provided for each of the nine body parts you will be exercising. (See individual exercises in Chapter 3.)

Resistance. The amount of weight used in a given exercise in order to challenge the muscle to "work."

Weight Progression. The periodic adding of weight to a given exercise as the weight being used becomes less of a challenge (due to the increasing strength of the exerciser). For example, in this workout, if you start out using ten-pound dumbbells for your biceps curl, chances are, in a month or two (or even sooner) you'll be using fifteen-pound dumbbells. It's necessary to increase your weights periodically in order to stimulate the muscle to growth.

Continual Pressure. The constant exertion of force on the working muscle. Continual contraction on the flexing part of the movement and constant tension on the stretching part of the movement provide a self-created force and can be more effective than the adding of heavier weights. In this workout, rather than asking you to progress to very heavy weights, we suggest that you exert full pressure as you exercise. In this way, you achieve quality (smaller, firmer muscles) rather than quantity (larger, bulkier muscles).

Definition. The description of a fully delineated or "defined" muscle due to the absence of surrounding body fat. Another term for definition is "muscularity," since the muscle is shown off at its best when well defined.

Density. The hardness of a muscle. Another way of expressing density is "firmness" or "tone," which is undoubtedly the goal of every woman. It is by exerting continual pressure on the working muscle rather than by lifting very heavy weights that density is achieved.

Equipment Vocabulary

This group of definitions describes your workout equipment, from the most basic to the most complex.

Flat Exercise Bench. A long, padded, narrow bench, parallel to the floor. Many flat exercise benches can be raised to an incline position (it's a good idea to purchase this type so you can do many exercise variations).

Free Weights. Barbells and dumbbells, which can be moved freely about the gym (as opposed to machines, which are stationary).

Dumbbell. A short metal bar with a weight on each end. Dumbbells are designed to be held in one hand.

Barbell. A long metal bar that holds weighted plates on each end. A barbell is designed to be held in two hands.

Plates. Disk-shaped weights that can be added to each end of the barbell. Such plates usually vary in weight from one and a quarter to forty-five pounds.

Collar. The holding device secured on each end of the barbell after the plates have been added to keep them from falling off. In order to save time many people do not use collars, but rather learn to be aware of the balancing of the weights on the barbell.

Exercise Machine. A device that exercises specific body parts. Machines are usually operated with pulleys or cams to control the weight resistance being applied. Machines are sometimes preferred over free weights for safety reasons, because the machine will literally "catch" the weight if you drop it. Machines are especially handy when working with extremely heavy weights. However, free weights are usually considered more effective in developing complete muscle tone, since with a free weight the exerciser must do all the work and there is less of a tendency to cheat. In certain instances, however, machines are preferable to free weights because they challenge the body part in a way that free weights cannot. These machines are: the lat pull-down machine, the pulley row machine, the leg-extension machine, and the leg-curl machine. However, there are excellent substitutes for these machines.

Whether you choose to use free weights or machines, you'll find that you experience a certain amount of soreness the day after working out.

Why Do Muscles Become Sore After Working Out?

It's normal to feel a certain amount of soreness from twenty-four to forty-eight hours after your first workout—and the more neglected the muscle has been, the more soreness you'll feel.

There are various theories as to why muscles become sore. Some experts believe that soreness is caused by lactic acid buildup. However, the truth is that lactic acid is long gone from the muscles by the time the soreness is apparent.

In addition, exercises that produce the most lactic acid are not the ones that cause the most soreness.

The soreness actually comes from the eccentric contraction of the muscles (the part of the exercise where you lower, rather than raise, the weight). This happens because the muscle fibers are being challenged to the maximum: They are lengthening, while at the same time they are attempting to contract. The end results of this work are minute tears in the muscle tissue itself. In addition, the muscle-tissue sheath becomes slightly stretched. When this happens, an imbalance of the collagen metabolism may occur. Finally, due to the osmotic pressure changes, a small amount of fluid is retained in the surrounding tissues. Any combination of these three factors can cause muscle soreness.

Another type of muscle soreness reveals itself in the form of an ache and occurs while you're working out. It happens when you're pushing your muscle beyond its present capacity. This type of pain is called "isochemic," and it occurs because your working muscle does not have enough oxygen to continue functioning at the level you're demanding of it. This ache disappears a few seconds after you stop forcing the muscle to work. The ache is harmless and is in fact often a good sign: It means that your muscles are being fully challenged.

Muscle soreness in general, whether it occurs during or after a workout, is not bad for your body, but rather is good for it. Without a certain amount of soreness when you first begin to work out, not much can be accomplished. Perhaps that's why the saying "No pain, no gain" was invented. However, in time the soreness will disappear—as the muscles become accustomed to the new workout. Every so often, however, if you work a little harder than usual, if you really go for the gusto, you may find yourself sore the next day.

Don't Let Soreness Stop You

Muscle soreness is not a signal to stop working out. You'll actually find that you feel better after a workout than you did before, because the workout itself functions to stretch out and massage the sore muscles.

If you're really sore and you want to do something to alleviate the discomfort before you start working out, you can do the warm-up stretches listed for the given exercises in a yogalike fashion. Instead of stretching in the usual manner (according to our stretch instructions), stretch the muscle until it feels tight, and hold it for about thirty seconds. Then slowly reduce the tension to the muscle.

Another way to relieve muscle soreness is to soak in a warm tub of water with about a half cup of Epsom salts. You can do this every night until the soreness goes away. The soreness should not last for more than two or three weeks.

The worst thing you could possibly do is totally stop exercising and wait until the soreness goes away. If you do this you'll only set yourself up for the same cycle of events again. The best thing is to continue to work out, adding the stretches when needed.

If you follow the appropriate "breaking-in-gently" plan (see Chapter 3) you should not experience unbearable soreness. If, on the other hand, you choose to ignore the instructions and plunge right in to a full thirty-minute alternate-day workout, you may find yourself in quite a bit of pain. Don't say I didn't warn you!

How Can You Tell the Difference Between Muscle Soreness and Injury?

If you pull a muscle and experience a twinge of pain, you'll know it right away. Soreness is pain on a much lower level. It comes after about twenty-four to forty-eight hours and will disappear after a time (depending upon the extent of the soreness after working out—anywhere from three days to a week). The pain that comes from injury, on the other hand, comes immediately and does not gradually disappear unless treated.

An example of an injury is a muscular tear. This can happen if you pull a weight too quickly or in an awkward manner. If this happens to you, you'll feel immediate and nearly incapacitating pain. For example, if you tear your quadriceps muscle, any kind of weight-bearing exercise to the leg will become extremely painful and will cause the muscle to "give out" and refuse to assist the body in carrying its weight.

Other common injuries are tendon and ligament injuries. All of these injuries require medical attention (braces, taping, pain-relief medication, etc.). If you think you're injured, check with your doctor immediately.

The good news is you'll be in little danger of injury as you follow this workout *if* you follow the exercise instructions carefully. Even though you'll be using relatively light weights, don't assume that you can't get injured. You must work in a calm, deliberate manner. Never jerk the weights or lurch from one position to the next. Never let the weights drop to the down position. Control them at all times. You'll note that we continually remind you, even nag you, about these things in our "Tips" sections.

Should You Stop Working Out if You Are Injured?

After you have consulted your doctor, work on whatever body parts you can still safely exercise, instead of completely stopping your workout. You may want to temporarily use *The Twelve-Minute Total-Body Workout* (see Bibliography) to keep yourself in shape while you're healing—with the permission of your doctor, of course.

Whatever you do, don't lie stagnant waiting to heal. Not only is this depressing—it slows down your healing. The more stimulation your body receives, the better your chances of healing quickly. In short, if you're injured, work around it, with the advice of your doctor.

Common Injuries in Weight Training and How to Avoid Them

Most injuries occur from incorrect technique, inflexibility, too much weight, or improper safety practices. If, however, you follow the exercise instructions, there should be no reason for injury. Using the proper technique as clearly instructed, you'll be flexible because you'll have performed the general body-part stretch indicated, and you'll have done a warm-up set without weights. You will not be lifting heavy weights, because you will have abided by our light-weight, gradual-break-in guidelines, and you'll be using proper safety practices as instructed.

Some of the most common weight-training injuries are: forearm tendon strains; forearm fractures; dislocated elbows; knee problems such as chondromalacia, meniscal tears, and patellar-tendon ruptures; head and neck injuries incurred due to excessive twisting; and shoulder injuries due to the lifting of heavy weights.

The reason many people become injured is simple. They begin a weight-training program without any clear idea of how to handle the weights properly. The correct technique requires a warm-up, prior to lifting weights, for the body part to be exercised. By doing a simple stretch before lifting, the muscles and joints are prepared for the workout, and tears, pulls, and strains to the muscles are avoided. In addition to a general body-part stretch for the particular muscle you're exercising, we will ask you to do a warm-up set for that body part with no weight. This is especially important, because it takes the muscle through the range of motion and provides the flexibility needed for lifting weights in that same range of motion.

A simple analogy can be made to a rubber band. A flexible rubber band can handle increased weight loads without breaking, while a tight or inflexible band will break or tear under strain. The point is, flexibility allows the lifter to handle weight without strain, and by taking the muscle through the range of motion without weight first, that flexibility is provided.

The position of the trunk, hands, and feet are extremely important in preventing injuries. Proper body mechanics will put less strain on the back, knees, and neck and evenly distribute the weight. Once again, we remind you to look at the photographs we provide and follow our simple instructions for each exercise.

Another common reason for injury is overzealousness. After working out for a few weeks, many people become overly excited and throw caution to the wind. They forget that adding weight to the overall routine must be done gradually (as instructed in Chapter 3), and they jump from a relatively light weight to a much heavier weight. Muscles must be prepared for increased weight. That is accomplished by gradually building up to heavier loads. Suddenly adding a huge amount of weight to a given exercise can put tremendous strain on tendons, ligaments, and muscles and can even cause rupture. If this happens, you'll experience excruciating pain and will have to give up working out with weights for an extended period of time (until the muscles are surgically repaired and the healing process is completed).

A final note on injury, though minor, involves the hands. Some people have very sensitive hands and form calluses easily. If this is you, be sure to wear lifting gloves. This idea may seem silly, especially since you'll be using relatively light weights. The truth is, it is quite unlikely that you'll get calluses from lifting three-, five-, ten-, or fifteen-pound dumbbells and twenty-five-pound barbells. However, just to be on the safe side, you might consider wearing gloves.

A Word About Body Types

Many women ask me about body types. They want to know if they are "mesomorphic" (ideal shape and size), "endomorphic" (fat), or "ectomorphic" (skinny) by nature. The truth is, although you may appear to be one body type at a given moment, and although you may have a proclivity toward a given body type because of your genetic makeup, with proper resistance training you can move toward the mesomorphic look. Let us first explain what body types are all about.

The main body types—endomorphic, mesomorphic, and ectomorphic—are called "somatotypes." The labels for these body types come from the terms "endomorphy" (fat makeup of the body), "mesomorphy" (muscle makeup of the body), and "ectomorphy" (the distribution of height to weight of the body).

As a person gains or loses weight, their endomorphy and ectomorphy inversely go up or down. Mesomorphy, on the other hand, seems to stay the same, except in the case where muscles atrophy due to disuse. Mesomorphy can be increased primarily by resistance training.

If this is true, it seems as if the whole idea of "body types" can be thrown out the window. Not true. As it turns out we are genetically coded to be inclined to go in one direction or another. We inherit a tendency toward a given body type. However, what we do about it will make all the difference. For example, if you tend to be naturally muscular (mesomorphic), but you vegetate instead of exercising and in addition you overeat, you'll soon look like an endomorph (fat).

You can figure out your present body type by following this prescription:

Endomorphy (rates fat makeup of the body): Are your contours rounded, and is your weight centered in the middle of your body?

Mesomorphy (rates relative strength and development of the muscular system): Is your body firm, well-formed, and contoured? Do you have no area where a large amount of fat is deposited?

Ectomorphy (rates the ratio of the distribution of weight to height): Do you have a smaller trunk, chest, and hips? Is your neck long and slender? Is your body weight low for your height? Is your frame thin and frail? Are you tall and do you have small wrists, ankles, knees, and elbow joints?

Endomorphy and mesomorphy change with the gain and loss of muscle and fat, but ectomorphy remains basically the same (you cannot change your bone structure or your height).

Chances are you think you're endomorphic now, but after you work out for a while you'll begin to appear more like a mesomorph. I don't see a need for you to spend hours mulling over your body type. In fact, we discourage identification with the negative endomorphic, fat type. Rather than claim a label, why not get working on a diet and exercise program that will gradually bring you to the look you want (increased muscle, less fat). This, and only this, use of somatotype labels is productive.

Now that you know how to do the workout and you're determined to get your body into its ideal shape, you'll need to decide where you want to work out.

You May Work Out at Home or at a Fitness Center: The Choice Is Yours

Working Out at Home

The main advantage of working out at home is, you're definitely going there—so there's a better chance you'll do your workout. No matter how well-intentioned we are, most of us are so busy and often so tired that the mere thought of going out of our way to get to a health club causes us to feel defeated and even depressed. "I don't have the time," we think. So instead of turning off on the highway, freeway, or street where the gym is located, we continue on and go straight home. Then, once we get there, we wish we had exercised self-discipline and gone to the gym. The end result is, we feel depressed and our workout is not accomplished.

There's good news. You can work out at home, and with excellent results. With a minimum of equipment (as described later on) that costs much less than one year's membership in any health spa, you can work in private, efficiently, and with no competition for the equipment. In addition, at home there will be no temptation to stop every five minutes and talk to other gym-goers.

If you do work out at home, however, you'll have to make sure you put on your telephone answering machine, ignore the doorbell, and let family members know that for thirty minutes, unless the world is ending, you're not to be disturbed.

Working Out at a Fitness Center

If you're so inclined, working out in a gym can be wonderful. It's inspiring to see other people exercising alongside you, and it's even more encouraging when someone says, "You're looking good. You've really made progress." Also, seeing other people sweating it out just like you helps you realize that it's not so bad after all. "We're all in the same boat," you say to yourself. "If you want the prize, you have to pay the price," you think, and you secretly pat yourself on the back for sticking with your workout plan.

Another advantage of working out in the gym is its variety of equipment. Certain gym machines, such as the lat pulldown machine, the pulley row machine, and the leg-extension and leg-curl machines, may be too expensive for home purchase and might be preferable to home workout substitutes.

In addition, working out in a well-equipped gym provides the opportunity to periodically switch from one type of exercise machine to another for a given body part. For example, if you work out in a gym you may want to do your bench press on a Universal gym machine for a while and later switch to the Nautilus press. After a while you may decide to work at the free-weight bench-press station. There are often three or more different style machines for each body part, and they are easily understood. And if you have a question, all you have to do is ask the gym attendant. The variety within an exercise itself can prevent boredom and the accompanying temptation to abandon your workout program.

All Things Considered

Although the ideal thing might be to go to a gym, many busy women feel that there are simply not enough hours in the day to travel to and from one, so they do their workout at home. If you're an idealist you may be saying, "Well, that's not so good because the perfect workout takes place in the gym." Not so. The perfect workout is the one that takes place consistently. What good is the perfect workout in the gym if it doesn't take place or if it takes place sporadically? Be honest with yourself. Which choice is more realistic for you? Better to work at home systematically without skipping workouts than to work in the gym on a hit-and-miss basis.

Equipment Needed if You Work Out at Home

If you choose to work out at home you'll need the following equipment, which can be purchased in any sporting-goods store.

A flat exercise bench (preferably one that can be raised to an incline). For a few dollars more you can get a bench with leg-extension, leg-curl, and bench-press attachments. It's a good idea to do this because it greatly expands your exercise possibilities—especially after working out for a while, when you are ready to do the alternates.

A set of:	3-lb. dumbbells *	(1-lb. dumbbells if
	5-lb. dumbbells *	you've never worked out
	8-lb. dumbbells	with weights before)
	10-lb. dumbbells	
	12-lb. dumbbells	
	15-lb. dumbbells	

If you want to be able to do all the alternate exercises (in time you may become tired of doing the same exercises), it's a good idea to purchase the following equipment too:

One:	15-lb. barbell
A set of:	2½-lb. plates
Two sets of:	5-lb. plates
A set of:	10-lb. plates

*Note: To begin, all you need is a pair of 3-lb. dumbbells, a pair of 5-lb. dumbbells, and a pair of 8-lb. dumbbells. The above weights are suggested because we know you'll eventually progress to the point where you need higher weights. You need not purchase them ahead of time. It's up to you.

Workout Clothing

When it comes to workout clothing, the simple rule of thumb is: comfort first, then beauty. Even if you work out at home where no one can see you, indulge yourself in workout clothing that is cheerful, flattering, and fun. After all, the most important person in the world still sees you at home—you. If you put on your husband's socks, your son's sweatpants, and a stained old blouse, there's no doubt you'll get depressed when you catch a glimpse of yourself in the mirror. Why not buy a couple of outfits that cheer you up? It could be a sweat outfit, a shorts and T-shirt ensemble, or a leotard. Suit your own personality. Pick your favorite colors. Let the clothing symbolize the way you feel about yourself.

3

The Thirty-Minute Workout

PART I:
How to Do the Workout

In order to get the promised results of a firm, strong, shapely body, you have to make a commitment to work with weights (do resistance training) for thirty minutes every other day. However, I don't expect you to start out by working out for thirty minutes every other day. Instead, I expect you to take it easy and break in gently, so you don't become so sore that you can't walk the next day and be tempted to quit.

If you relax and follow my advice, you'll be more than able to cope with the workout in a matter of weeks. In the following pages you'll find three "break-in-gently" plans. The first, "beginners," is for those who have little or no experience with weight training. The second, "intermediate," is for those who have some experience with weight training, but who have not been consistent in their training or who haven't worked out with weights in the past six months. The third, "advanced," is for those quite familiar with weight training and who have been working out with weights regularly for over a year.

Before you decide which break-in plan you're going to use, take a look at what your alternate-day thirty-minute workout will look like once you are in full swing.

The Overall Workout

You'll be exercising one half of your body—chest, shoulders, triceps, abdominals, and calves—on Workout Day 1, resting one day, then exercising the other half of your body—thighs, hips/buttocks, back, and biceps—on Workout Day 2. You'll rest a day, go back to the first half of your body, and so on. Here's how your workout breaks down. (You'll notice the exercise chapters are also in this order, for your convenience.)

WORKOUT DAY 1:	WORKOUT DAY 2:
Chest	Thighs
Shoulders	Hips/Buttocks
Triceps	Back
Abdominals	Biceps
Calves	

On the given workout days, you'll eventually do three sets each of the following exercises for each body part.

THIRTY-MINUTE WORKOUT

DAY 1

CHEST

Wing stretch
Flat dumbbell press
Flat dumbbell flye
Cross-bench pullover

SHOULDERS

The shrug stretch
Standing alternate shoulder press
Side lateral raise
Front lateral raise
Seated rear-deltoid raise

TRICEPS

Cross-face triceps-extension stretch
Cross-face triceps extension
Standing double-arm overhead triceps extension
Double-arm kickback

ABDOMINALS

The circle stretch
Crunch
Knee-up
Floor side-bend
Sit-up with a twist

CALVES

Achilles stretch
Seated calf raise
Standing calf raise

Now you should rest for one day. You may do some walking, engage in a favorite sport or aerobic activity, or just relax. (See Chapter 4 for alternate-day aerobic and sports suggestions.)

THIRTY-MINUTE WORKOUT

—— DAY **2** ——

Now you are ready to exercise the other half of your body. Here are the specific exercises you will do for each body part.

THIGHS
Quadriceps stretch
Dumbbell squat
Dumbbell lunge
Sissy squat

HIPS AND BUTTOCKS
Bent-knee bottom-pull stretch
Side leg lift
Kneeling kickback
Hip raise
Seated scissors
Lying scissors

BACK
Bent-knee back stretch
Bent dumbbell row
Seated back lateral
One-arm dumbbell bent row

BICEPS
Behind-back arm-lift stretch
Concentration curl
Standing alternate hammer curl
Standing alternate biceps curl

Warm-up Stretching Before the Workout

You'll find suggested stretches in the specific body-part chapters. You should take advantage of them before beginning your workout for that body part. The warm-up stretch does not take more than a minute or two and will be well worth your time—as insurance against injury. Also, it's a good idea to end your workout by doing the warm-up stretch again.

Sets and Repetitions

Do three sets of ten repetitions for each exercise. (See Chapter 2 for a review of "set" and "repetition.")

How Much Weight Should You Use?

Some body parts are stronger than others. You'll find that your chest, calves, thighs, back, and biceps can handle more weight than your shoulders and triceps. Notice that the workout for the buttocks and abdominals requires no weight. This will be explained later.

Unless you're an experienced bodybuilder, we suggest you start out with the following weights. (All the exercises require dumbbells. Barbells are used only for the alternate exercises):

Chest Calves	5-lb. dumbbells or 15-lb. barbell where applicable
Thighs Back and Biceps Shoulders Triceps	1- or 3-lb. dumbbells, depending upon how strong you are
Buttocks Abdominals	No weight. Instead, eventually build up to 25 repetitions per set. Then use a maximum of a 3- to 5-lb. ankle weight or a 3- to 5-lb. dumbbell. See specific exercise instructions

Increasing the Weight

After about a month of working out you may find that the weight you're using is too light. If this is so, move up to the next weight.

For example, if you're using three-pound dumbbells for your shoulder exercises and they become too easy (you find yourself able to do more than ten perfect repetitions), advance to five-pound dumbbells. At first you may not be able to get more than five repetitions. That's fine. After all, you're getting adjusted to a new weight.

Chances are, you'll be able to do at least six repetitions, because you'll have gotten stronger. The fact that you can do ten repetitions so easily with the three-pound weights demonstrates that fact.

It's not a good idea to skip a weight and advance too quickly up the scale, because you may become sloppy and sacrifice form in order to cope with the added weight. In addition, you run the risk of injury. In other words, we do not suggest that you go from three-pound dumbbells for your shoulder exercises to ten-pound dumbbells. Take it in steps. Be wise and play it safe.

Now that you know exactly what the thirty-minute alternate-day workout is all about, here are your "break-in-gently" instructions.

Beginner Break-in Program

If you're badly out of shape and have little or no experience in resistance training (working with weights), you should follow the beginner break-in program. Always do the stretch for each exercise before you begin to exercise each body part.

Do a warm-up set with no weights for each exercise first.

Week 1
1 set of each exercise with 1-lb. weights

Week 2
2 sets of each exercise with 1-lb. weights

Week 3
3 sets of each exercise with 1-lb. weights

Week 4
1 set of each exercise with 1-lb. weights
2 sets of each exercise with 3-lb. weights

Week 5
3 sets of each exercise with 3-lb. weights

Week 6
1 set of each exercise with 3-lb. weights
2 sets of each exercise with weights as described on p. 33

Week 7
Full program using weights as described on pp. 33–34

The purpose of doing the exercises with very little weight for the first three weeks is to help you become accustomed to exercising each of your body parts without the strain of resistance. It is also to help you become accustomed to doing the exercises in strict form so that you won't develop any bad habits. If we asked you to use heavier weights too soon, you'd become preoccupied with the burden of the work and might be tempted to cheat. You may end up doing half repetitions, resting between repetitions, jerking and lurching the weights, letting them nearly drop to the start position—all of the things I continually warn you against in the "Tips" sections.

The Purpose of the Warm-up Set

The warm-up set takes your muscle through the intended range of motion and prepares it for the workout. This weightless set serves to loosen the muscle, increase the muscle temperature, and increase the volume of blood flowing through it. You'll continue to do a warm-up set without weights forever for each exercise you do.

Intermediate Break-in Program

If you've worked out with weights before, but haven't been consistent in your training or haven't worked out with weights in the past six months, I suggest you follow the intermediate break-in program.

Do a warm-up set with no weights for each exercise first.

Week 1
3 sets of each exercise with 1-lb. weights

Week 2
2 sets of each exercise with 1-lb. weights
1 set of each exercise with 3-lb. weights

Week 3
1 set of each exercise with 3-lb. weights
2 sets of each exercise with weights as described earlier

Week 4
3 sets of each exercise with weights as described earlier

Advanced Break-in Program

If you've been working out with weights on a regular basis, we suggest you follow this break-in program. It may be tempting for you to simply begin by doing all three sets of each exercise—and skipping the break-in period entirely. Since we don't know exactly what you've been doing in your weight-training sessions, we can't let you do that with our blessing. If you choose to ignore the advanced break-in program and just start out with a full thirty-minute program, you do so at your own risk. Don't misunderstand. I'm not implying that we believe you'll become injured if you do this. I'm simply saying that because I don't know your history, I can't recommend it.

Here's what I suggest for an advanced break-in program.

Do a warm-up set with no weights for each exercise first.

Week 1
1 set of each exercise with 3-lb. weights
1 set of each exercise with weights as described earlier

Week 2
1 set of each exercise with 3-lb. weights
2 sets of each exercise with weights as described earlier

Week 3
3 sets of each exercise with weights as described earlier

The Purpose of the Break-in Program

Whether you're a beginner, an intermediate, or an advanced weight-trainee, it's a good idea to follow a break-in program for three reasons:

1) You allow yourself time to learn the exercises so you can perform them in strict form. Your workout will take only ten minutes, if that, for the first week. However, since you have the extra time, slow down and take the additional time required to learn the exercise movements.
2) If you learn to perform the exercises in strict form from day one, you'll gain more from the overall program. Remember, we can only guarantee the results if you follow the exercises exactly as prescribed.
3) By taking it easy, one step at a time, you lessen the chances of becoming discouraged or overwhelmed. It's amazing what can be accomplished if you have the patience to go one step at a time.

Pre-strengthening Exercises

You'll notice that I include special strengthening exercises in the hips and buttocks section and the back section. I've included these pre-strengthening exercises for those of you who feel that your muscles are extremely weak in these areas. If you're not sure, do them anyway. They take only a few minutes and can help to make your regular workout that much more enjoyable.

Review of Your Workout

Once you've broken in gently, follow the workout plan as described in the beginning of this chapter. You'll exercise five body parts on Workout Day 1 and four body parts on Workout Day 2.

For each exercise you'll be doing three sets of ten repetitions. But before you begin your set with weights, you will always do a quick warm-up set for the body part you're exercising. You could say you're doing four sets in all—one without weights, and three with weights. It's the weightless set that helps prevent injury by taking the muscle through the range of motion.

Advanced Techniques

What about those of you who want to go the extra mile, who are willing to invest more time? There are a variety of advanced techniques found in Chapter 4, "Optional Extras." In it you'll find advanced techniques and additional exercise suggestions that will allow you to work out for up to an hour or slightly more. You'll also note in that chapter that because this workout is based upon the "split routine" (see Chapter 2 for a review), if you so choose you may work out every day, giving yourself only one day off a week! But that's only for those of you who want to push yourselves to the limit.

Fitting the Program into Your Schedule

You'll be working with weights every other day for thirty minutes. It's up to you to decide whether or not you're an "owl" or a "lark." An owl does better working later in the day, while a lark, the early bird, does better getting up at the crack of dawn and giving it her first thrust of energy. There's another group who function best when they can seize upon any fragment of time and squeeze their workout in. They see it as a challenge. These people can be called "vultures," because they land on a chance to use time wisely and they make the best of the moment. Not a minute of time is wasted. Such people can work out for a half hour during their lunch break or can work out at different times during the day in a given week—whenever they can fit it in. They don't need a set schedule. One day it can be in the morning, another at lunch, and another late at night.

An Alternate Plan: Working Out Three Days a Week Instead of Every Other Day

It's very possible that the idea of working out every other day does not appeal to you because it does not enable you to line up a set workout schedule, say, "Mondays, Wednesdays, and Fridays," or "Tuesdays, Thursdays, and Saturdays."

If you prefer having your workout days nailed down, there's no reason why you can't work out on a set three days a week. After all, in doing this you'll only be working out two days less in a four-week period. (Four weeks equals twenty-eight days. Working out every other day would entail working out fourteen of the twenty-eight days. Working out three days a week would entail working out three times four, or twelve, days. If missing the two days bothers you, you could always add them into the four weeks anywhere you please. You have the option of doing this since you are on a split routine.)

Using the Variations

After about three months you may choose to do some of the exercise variations instead of the regular exercises. The advantage of this is twofold: You ensure a well-balanced muscular development because the muscle is challenged in a slightly different way, and you prevent boredom and the temptation to quit.

Making Up a Skipped Workout

It's not a good idea to skip a workout—especially in the beginning stages (the first eight weeks). If you do, however, you can work two days in a row to make up the missed workout and then resume your alternate-day schedule.

A second option, if you know you're going to be busy ahead of time, is working ahead. For example, if you work out on Monday, have free time on Tuesday, but know you're going to be busy Wednesday, why not work ahead and do your Wednesday workout on Tuesday? Then you can have Wednesday off. On Thursday you can resume your regular alternate-day workout. "But won't I really be working extra this way?" you may ask. Yes. A little extra if we figured it out mathematically, but so what? All the better. It won't hurt you and it can certainly help you. Better to be one step ahead of the game than a half step behind.

Following the Order and Sequence of the Exercises

As mentioned in Chapter 2, our workout is not a hit-or-miss conglomeration of exercises. It has been tested and proved to work—if, and only if, you follow it exactly. If you are going to skip around and do, say, one chest exercise, an abdominal exercise, a shoulder exercise, and then a triceps exercise, you'll be violating the basic Weider principle of muscle isolation. As mentioned before, in order for a muscle to be challenged to its ideal shape and growth, it must be stimulated to a certain level before an extended rest period.

If you wish, you may change the order of the particular body parts within a workout day. For example, on Workout Day 1 you may want to begin your workout with abdominals instead of the chest. Why? You may hate working the abdominals and wish to get it out of the way first. This isn't a problem. However, since the chest and shoulders are directly related to each other, you should exercise them in sequence. Any other body part can be interchanged. For Workout Day 2 it's a good idea to exercise thighs and buttocks in sequence, because those two body parts are interrelated.

If you choose to change the order of the workout, it's a good idea to get the most difficult or troublesome body part out of the way first, so you can devote your first and greatest thrust of energy to it. That way, you won't dread working on it during your routine.

Why the Buttocks and Abdominals Require Little or No Weight and High Repetitions

The buttocks and abdominals are traditionally exercised with little or no weight and high repetitions. Why?

The buttocks is a large muscle to begin with. The last thing you want to do is use heavy weights to make it larger. In order to tighten and tone the buttocks, the best thing is to use no weight or light weights and eventually build up to three sets of twenty-five repetitions each. This way you'll tighten and tone the buttocks muscle without making it bigger.

The abdominal muscles are long and segmented. They respond to high repetitions and little or no weight better than to low repetitions and high weight. Your ultimate goal will be to build up to three sets of twenty-five repetitions each on all abdominal exercises.

Building Up to Three Sets of Twenty-Five Repetitions on Buttocks and Abdominal Exercises

You'll start out doing three sets of ten repetitions each for your buttocks and abdominal muscles—if you can even do ten repetitions at first. If you can't, don't despair. Just do what you can, and add one repetition every week or two until you reach twenty-five per set—even if it takes a year. There's no rush. Take your time. You'll be amazed at how much you can accomplish if you are patient.

Many women can't do more than one or two repetitions per set of abdominal exercises in the beginning. In a year's time these very women are doing three sets of twenty-five repetitions. What would have happened if they began to criticize themselves just because they couldn't get off the ground for more than two repetitions during the first two weeks?

The fact is, if you persist you'll eventually get stronger. It's inevitable. Slowly, slowly—the mountain is climbed, the battle is won. The old saying "Rome wasn't built in a day" may be timeworn, but it holds a comforting truth. Everything in its time.

For Inspiration and Further Information

Don't just stop here. Keep yourself inspired and informed by subscribing to magazines offering the latest information on diet, nutrition, and exercise. *Shape* and *Muscle and Fitness* magazines are excellent sources of information, but what's more, they regularly include success stories of women who have overcome seemingly overwhelming obstacles and gotten into shape. I have a regular column in both these magazines. Women from all over the United States and Europe write to me, and I respond to them in these columns. I would love to hear from you, too, as you share your concerns and your successes.

PART II:
Workout Day One—
Chest, Shoulders,
Triceps, Abdominals,
and Calves

**UPLIFTING THE
BREASTS**

Chest muscles can make all the difference on a woman. Although you can't do much to make your breasts larger (short of simply getting fat), you *can* make them appear fuller, firmer, and higher.

By working out with weights the right way you can develop your pectoral muscles. These muscles are located under the breasts and when developed serve as an undergirding or foundation for them. In addition, working with weights can help create muscular separation of the breasts, or "cleavage." All of this helps to give the breasts a more shapely, youthful look.

The breasts themselves are not muscles, but glands weighing anywhere from a half pound to four pounds each and varying in size, depending upon genetics. The weight of each breast is held in place by the skin, the Cooper's ligament (a ligament consisting of fiberlike chains that attach to the skin internally and allow the breast to have sufficient motion), and the pectoral muscles.

Why Do Breasts Sag as a Woman Ages and What Can Be Done About It?

Breasts sag on some women more than others. Small-breasted women sag less than large-breasted women, because there is less pressure from the sheer force of gravity pulling the breasts downward. Pregnancy and breast-feeding will also contribute to sagging, because during these times the breasts are enlarged. When pregnancy and breast-feeding are over and the breasts return to normal size, they'll have lost some of their elasticity and will be slightly stretched. Naturally, the more pregnancies and the more breast-feeding, the greater the stretching and sagging.

In addition, the breasts naturally sag as a woman gets older. Each year after thirty, the skin and the Cooper's ligament stretch and the pectoral muscles atrophy.

While nothing can be done about the stretching of the Cooper's ligament and the skin (short of a breast-lift operation or breast implants), something very specific can be done about the atrophying pectoral muscles. They can be built up to support the breasts. While this will not completely eliminate the sagging, it will do a lot to improve the look of the breasts.

When a woman approaches the age of fifty-five, yet another factor enters into the picture. Menopause causes internal changes in the breast structure. Since the breasts' function as a mammary gland is no longer needed, the glandular tissues begin to decrease and fat begins to gradually take over, causing the breasts to become less firm.

All things considered, the best way to reduce the sagging and increase the firmness of the breasts is to work with weights as described in the following pages.

Before you begin your chest routine it's a good idea to understand the basic workings of the pectoral (chest) muscles.

Muscle Description

The chest consists of three major muscle groups: the intercostals, the pectoralis major, and the serratus anterior.

The intercostals are located between each pair of ribs and form a layered arrangement—external and internal—at right angles to each other.

These muscles function to help you inhale and raise the ribs as you do so. They are especially important when

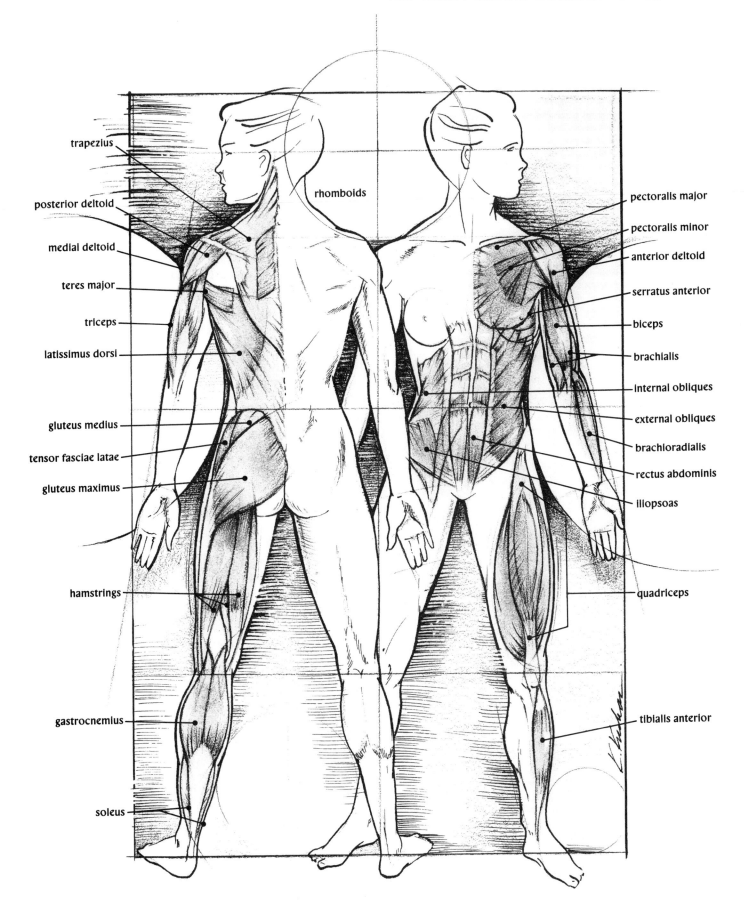

trapezius

posterior deltoid

medial deltoid

teres major

triceps

latissimus dorsi

gluteus medius

tensor fasciae latae

gluteus maximus

hamstrings

gastrocnemius

soleus

rhomboids

pectoralis major

pectoralis minor

anterior deltoid

serratus anterior

biceps

brachialis

internal obliques

external obliques

brachioradialis

rectus abdominis

iliopsoas

quadriceps

tibialis anterior

you're engaged in activities that cause you to breathe deeply.

The intercostal muscles are developed and strengthened every time you inhale deeply.

The pectoralis major is a two-headed, fan-shaped muscle that lies across the front of the upper chest. The clavicular head is the small head, and it forms the upper pectoral area. The sternal head is the larger head, and it forms the lower pectoral area. The pectoralis muscle originates at the collarbone and runs along the breastbone to the cartilage connecting the upper ribs to the breastbone.

The pectoralis major functions to flex the chest and to pull the upper arm down and across the body. This muscle is developed by the flat dumbbell press, the flat dumbbell flye, and the cross-bench pullover.

The serratus anterior originates along the outer surface of the eight upper ribs and connects to the underside of the shoulder blade near the spinal column.

The serratus anterior functions to stabilize the shoulder girdle when an upward movement is performed. It is strengthened and developed by the flat dumbbell press and the cross-bench pullover.

Before you begin your chest routine it's a good idea to perform a general chest stretch.

Chest Routine

Wing Stretch

This stretch relaxes and elongates the pectoral muscles. It also helps stretch out the shoulder muscles, especially the rear deltoid.

✦ **POSITION**

Stand erect with your feet in a natural position and your back straight, looking straight ahead. Raise your elbows until your upper arms are parallel to the floor, and let your clenched fists touch each other at the center of your upper chest.

✦ **STRETCH**

Pull your elbows back as far as possible, until you feel a full stretch in your chest muscles. Hold the position for three seconds.

✦ **TIMING**

Perform the stretch three times.

TIPS   Beware of the temptation to jerk your elbows back as you perform this movement. You will get much more out of the stretch if you maintain a steady, fluid motion. Keep your mind on your pectoral (chest) muscles as you stretch.

Chest Exercise #1
Flat Dumbbell Press

~~~~~~

The flat dumbbell press strengthens, shapes, and defines the pectoral and serratus anterior muscles. It helps build an underlying muscle that uplifts the breast, and it strengthens the triceps muscle as well. The advantage of using dumbbells as opposed to a barbell is the ability to strictly control the movement and to allow for a full range of motion.

✦ **POSITION**

Lie flat on your back on an exercise bench with a dumbbell held in each hand at each armpit, knuckles facing upward.

✦ **MOVEMENT**

Keeping your elbows relatively close to your body, extend your arms straight up, and flex (squeeze) your pectoral muscles as you go. Return to start position. Make sure you lower the dumbbells as far as possible, and feel a full stretch in your chest. Repeat the movement until you have completed your set.

✦ **TIPS**

Beware of the tendency to tense your neck. Consciously relax your neck while you are working.

Keep the working dumbbells even with each other.

Keep your back flat on the bench.

✦ **VARIATIONS**

You may do this exercise on an incline bench for greater emphasis on the upper pectoral muscle. You may perform this exercise in a gym at a bench-press station, with a barbell. You may perform this exercise on any gym bench-press machine (a barbell-type device will be substituted for the dumbbells).

Flat dumbbell press, start

Flat dumbbell press, finish

Chest Exercise #2
Flat Dumbbell Flye

~~~~~~

The flat dumbbell flye strengthens and shapes the pectoral and serratus anterior muscles. It creates a separation between the breasts and develops a look of "cleavage."

✦ **POSITION**

Lie flat on your back on an exercise bench with a dumbbell in each hand, arms extended straight up and palms facing each other. Bend your elbows slightly and let the dumbbells touch each other in the center of your body.

✦ **MOVEMENT**

Extend your arms outward and downward in a semicircular movement until you feel a complete stretch in your pectoral muscles. Return to start position and flex (squeeze) your chest muscles. Repeat the movement until you have completed your set.

✦ **TIPS**

Beware of the tendency to arch your back and rise from the bench. Keep your back flat on the bench at all times.

Remember to keep your elbows slightly bent throughout the exercise.

✦ **VARIATION**

You may perform this exercise on an incline bench for greater emphasis on the upper pectoral muscles.

Flat dumbbell flye, start

Flat dumbbell flye, finish

Chest Exercise #3
Cross-Bench Pullover

The cross-bench pullover helps to shape and strengthen the pectoral and serratus anterior muscles. In addition, it stretches and expands the rib cage and straightens the latissimus dorsi muscles.

✦ **POSITION**

Place your shoulders on the edge of an exercise bench and hold one dumbbell in both hands, knuckles facing upward and thumbs interlocked. Extend your arms straight up so that the dumbbell is held directly above your chin area. Knees bent, plant your feet flat on the ground and keep your buttocks low.

✦ **MOVEMENT**

Lower the dumbbell behind you until you cannot go any farther, bending your elbows and extending your arms over and behind your head. Stretch your pectoral muscles and return to start position. Flex (squeeze) your chest muscles. Repeat the movement until you have completed your set.

✦ **TIPS**

Continually focus your mind on your pectoral muscles as you stretch and flex that area.

✦ **VARIATION**

You may perform this exercise with a lighter weight, one arm at a time. If you do this, be sure to continually bring your working raised arm back to the area at the center of your chest.

Summary of Chest Exercises

PRE-WORKOUT STRETCH

Wing

CHEST ROUTINE

Flat dumbbell press
Flat dumbbell flye
Cross-bench pullover

Cross-bench pullover, start

Cross-bench pullover, finish

DEFINING THE SHOULDERS

The shoulders help give a woman's upper body a soft, feminine look: Their roundness helps her wear clothing in a flattering way. A woman with well-shaped shoulders won't have to depend upon padding to help her appear well-balanced. She won't have to worry about her shoulders disappearing when she wears a strapless dress.

The shoulders help you appear upright and strong, as opposed to slumped and stooped. Without adequately developed shoulder and trapezius muscles a woman will have a scrawny neck and shoulder look, adding age to her appearance.

Well-shaped shoulders improve posture as well as carriage. There's no two ways about it. If you want to look young and beautiful you can't afford to neglect developing and strengthening your shoulders.

Exercising the shoulders helps keep the muscles and connective tissues in that area flexible and supple, decreasing the chance of the onset of rheumatism. If you already have rheumatism in your shoulder area, exercising as prescribed in this chapter can help alleviate your pain, because much of the stiffness will be eliminated by the carefully designed movements of each specific exercise.

Before you begin your shoulder workout it's a good idea to understand the basic workings of those muscles.

Muscle Description

The deltoid (shoulder) is a triangular muscle. It resembles an inverted version of the Greek letter "delta" and, like the letter, has three parts that function independently or as a group. The three parts are called the anterior (front deltoid), the medial (middle or side deltoid), and the posterior (rear deltoid).

The entire deltoid muscle originates at the upper extreme of the shoulder blade and connects to the collarbone. The three parts of the muscle weave together and insert on the bone of the upper arm. They fall over the shoulder area in this fashion: One angle points down the arm, while the other two angles weave around to the front and back.

The anterior part of the deltoid muscle works in conjunction with the pectoral muscles to lift the arm and move it forward. The medial part of the muscle works to lift the arm sideways. The posterior part of the muscle works in conjunction with the latissimus dorsi and teres major to extend the arm backward.

The deltoid muscles are used in most day-to-day body movements. For example, we use our deltoid muscles every time we lift something from the floor, carry a suitcase or bag of groceries, raise a hand high, or even swing our arms when walking.

The standing alternate shoulder press, the side lateral raise, and the front lateral raise all work to strengthen, shape, and develop all three areas of the deltoid muscle. However, certain exercises emphasize one area more than the others (see specific exercises).

Before you begin your shoulder routine it's a good idea to do a general shoulder stretch.

Shoulder Routine

The Shrug Stretch

This stretch relaxes the entire deltoid (shoulder) area.

◆ **POSITION**

Stand with your feet a natural width apart, your arms down at your sides in a relaxed position, and look straight ahead.

◆ **STRETCH**

Slowly raise your shoulders as high as possible. Then pull them back as far as you can, stretch them down, and then back to start position (the stretch follows a backward circular motion).

◆ **TIMING**

Repeat the stretch three times. There's no need to stop between stretches; just continue to circle up and back until you have fulfilled the required number of repetitions.

◆ **TIPS**

You may relax your neck further by doing the following: Gently let your head fall forward until your chin drops as low as possible. Return your head to the upright position, then gently let your head drop to your right shoulder as far as possible. Return to head-upright position, and gently let your head drop toward your back as far as possible. Again return to start, and gently let your head drop toward your left shoulder as far as possible. Hold each position for about six seconds.

Realize that you are not "rolling" your neck. You are stretching your neck in four directions. You'll find that in time, you'll be able to stretch your neck farther and farther. Do not force the stretch. You should never feel pain when doing this stretch.

Shoulder Exercise #1
Standing Alternate Shoulder Press

~~~~~~

The shoulder press strengthens, shapes, and defines the entire deltoid area. In addition, the triceps and trapezius muscles are strengthened.

◆ **POSITION**

Stand with your feet a natural width apart, and hold a dumbbell in each hand at shoulder height, palms facing up.

◆ **MOVEMENT**

Extend your right arm upward until you can't go any higher. As you begin returning to start position, start to extend your left arm upward. When your left arm reaches its highest point, your right arm should have returned to start position. Continue this alternating movement until you have completed your set.

◆ **TIPS**

Do not rock from side to side. Keep your body steady.

Flex (squeeze) your deltoid muscles on the up movement and stretch them on the down movement.

◆ **VARIATIONS**

You may perform this exercise with a barbell to the front (military press to the front) or a barbell to the rear (military press to the rear).

Standing alternate shoulder press, start

Standing alternate shoulder press, finish

Shoulder Exercise #2
Side Lateral Raise

~~~~~~

The side lateral raise strengthens, shapes, and defines the entire shoulder area, with a special emphasis on the middle, or medial, deltoid muscle.

◆ **POSITION**

Stand with your feet a natural width apart and hold a dumbbell in each hand, palms facing each other, the dumbbells touching in the center of your body.

◆ **MOVEMENT**

Lock your wrists and raise the dumbbells out to your sides (keeping your elbows slightly bent) until they reach shoulder height. Flex (squeeze) your shoulder muscles, and return to start position. Feel the stretch in your shoulder muscles. Repeat the movement until you have completed your set.

◆ **TIPS**

Do not lock your elbows. Keep them slightly bent throughout the exercise.

Curve your wrists slightly inward and lock them throughout the movement.

Never jerk the weights outward or let them drop to start position. Maintain control at all times.

◆ **VARIATION**

You may perform this exercise one arm at a time, holding on to a support with your free arm.

Side lateral raise, start

Side lateral raise, finish

Shoulder Exercise #3
Front Lateral Raise

~~~~~~

The front lateral raise strengthens, shapes, and defines the entire shoulder area, with a special emphasis on the front (anterior) deltoid muscle.

✦ **POSITION**

Stand with your feet a natural width apart and hold a dumbbell in each hand, palms facing your body. Keep your arms straight and let the dumbbells touch the center of your thighs.

✦ **MOVEMENT**

Lock your elbows and raise the dumbbells straight out in front until they reach shoulder height. Flex (squeeze) your shoulder muscle and return to start position. Feel the stretch in your shoulder muscles. Repeat the movement until you have completed your set.

✦ **TIPS**

Do not swing the dumbbells up and down. Maintain full control at all times.

✦ **VARIATIONS**

You may perform this exercise by alternating one arm at a time.

You may perform this exercise with a barbell.

Front lateral raise, start   **Front lateral raise, finish**

Shoulder Exercise #4
Seated Rear-Deltoid Raise

This exercise strengthens, shapes, and defines the rear-deltoid muscles. Strong rear-deltoid muscles help improve your posture.

✦ **POSITION**

Sit at the edge of a flat exercise bench with a dumbbell in each hand, palms facing your body. Lean forward until your chest is nearly touching your thighs. Bring the dumbbells together under your bent legs, nearly touching them together.

✦ **MOVEMENT**

Keeping your elbows only slightly bent, extend your arms outward until nearly parallel to the floor. Flex your rear-deltoid muscles and return to start position. Without resting, repeat the movement until you have completed your set.

✦ **TIPS**

Concentrate on your rear-deltoid muscles while you move the dumbbells up and down. Flex on the upward movement, and feel the stretch on the downward movement.

Be aware of the temptation to swing the dumbbells up and to let them drop nearly to start position. This is your body trying to get out of the work. Don't give in. Maintain strict, slow, deliberate movements.

✦ **VARIATION**

You may perform this exercise standing, by bending your body until your torso is nearly parallel to the floor.

Summary of Shoulder Exercises

PRE-WORKOUT STRETCH
The shrug

SHOULDER ROUTINE
Standing alternate shoulder press
Side lateral raise
Front lateral raise
Seated rear-deltoid raise

Seated rear-deltoid raise, start

Seated rear-deltoid raise, finish

Standing rear-deltoid raise, start (Variation)

Standing rear-deltoid raise, finish (Variation)

TIGHTENING THE TRICEPS

The dreaded triceps. The part of a woman's arm that gives away her age—if she isn't smart enough to do a few simple exercises to remedy the problem.

Your triceps muscle is located on your upper arm, opposite your biceps. It's the most neglected muscle on the female body, because it's not called on to do work on a regular basis. You can tell if your triceps is out of shape by extending your arm straight out in front of you, with your thumb facing forward, and swinging your arm back and forth in a quick motion. Question: Does your triceps area wave back and forth, or is it firm and stable? Is your triceps area composed mainly of fat and hanging skin, or does it have a firm, shapely muscle?

Don't despair. We can help you. In a few months you'll see a dramatic improvement in this area. You'll notice that the skin that was formerly loose is now taut, because a firm, shapely muscle has been developed underneath it. You will also notice that the triceps is now firm to the touch, because instead of fat deposits under the skin you now have a hard-earned muscle.

Age will not limit your progress. As mentioned before, it may take a fifty-year-old woman a little longer to develop a firm triceps muscle than it takes a twenty-five-year-old, but not *that* much longer—a matter of weeks or, at most, a couple of months longer. So what?

The only thing that can stop you from developing a firm, shapely triceps is lethargy. If you refuse to do the exercises prescribed in this chapter in a consistent manner, you will not achieve your goal. If, on the other hand, you follow the instructions exactly, exercise your triceps muscle with challenging weights as described in Chapter 4, and remember to increase your weights as the exercise becomes too easy with the weight you're using, you'll see amazing progress.

While we're on the subject of bodybuilders, let us assure you that if you follow this workout you will not develop a gigantic triceps muscle. The myth that the moment you pick up a weight your body will spring forth bulky muscles was dispelled long ago. Extensive research has proved that men develop larger muscles because they have higher levels of the hormone testosterone (about twenty to thirty times higher) than women.

So no more excuses. The only way you can tighten and tone your triceps muscle is do the correct resistance exercises to stimulate the muscle fibers to lengthen and strengthen. Let's go to work, ladies!

Before you begin your workout, however, it's a good idea to become familiar with the physiology and function of the triceps muscle.

Muscle Description

The triceps is a three-headed muscle. The two shorter heads are attached to the back side of the upper arm bone (humerus) near the elbow. The longer head is attached to the shoulder blade. The longer head functions differently than the two shorter heads: It pulls the arm back once it moves away from the body. The other two heads, in conjunction with the longer head, work to extend the arm and forearm.

The cross-face triceps extension, the double-arm overhead triceps extension, and the double-arm kickback all work to tighten, tone, and strengthen the entire triceps muscle.

Before you begin your triceps routine it's a good idea to do a general triceps stretch.

Triceps Routine

Cross-Face Triceps Extension Stretch

This stretch relaxes the entire triceps area.

✦ **POSITION**

Stand straight with knees bent and with your feet a natural width apart and your arms down at your sides.

✦ **STRETCH**

Bend slightly forward at the waist, keeping your upper arms close to your body, and extend your arms out behind you as far back as possible. Feel the stretch in your triceps muscle.

✦ **TIMING**

Perform three three-second stretches.

✦ **TIPS**

Keep your upper arms close to your body throughout the movement.

It's easy to forget which muscle you're stretching with this movement. Keep your mind focused on the triceps muscle as you perform this stretch.

Triceps Exercise #1
Cross-Face Triceps Extension

～～～～～～～～～～～～～～～～～～～～～～

The cross-face triceps extension strengthens, shapes, and tightens the entire triceps muscle, especially the inner area.

✦ **POSITION**

Holding a dumbbell in your right arm, lie flat on an exercise bench. Extend your right arm straight up, palm facing your body. Turn your face toward your right arm so your chin is touching your shoulder.

✦ **MOVEMENT**

Bending your arm at the elbow, lower your right arm until your fist touches your left ear. Return to start position and flex (squeeze) your triceps muscle. Repeat the movement until you have completed your set. Repeat the set for the other arm.

✦ **TIPS**

Maintain the averted-face position throughout the exercise.

Place your nonworking fingers on your working triceps muscle so you can gauge the intensity of your flexing and stretching.

✦ **VARIATION**

You may perform this exercise on an incline bench.

Cross-face triceps extension, start

Cross-face triceps extension, finish

Triceps Exercise #2

Standing Double-Arm Overhead Triceps Extension

The triceps extension strengthens, shapes, and tones the entire triceps muscle, especially the inner and middle heads of the muscle.

✦ **POSITION**

Stand with your feet a natural width apart and hold a dumbbell above your head, arms extended straight up. Your hands should hold the dumbbell balanced between your thumbs and interlocked fingers, palms facing upward. Keep your biceps as close to your head as possible throughout the exercise.

✦ **MOVEMENT**

Bending at the elbows, lower the dumbbell behind you until it touches your upper back. Flexing (squeezing) your triceps muscles as hard as possible, return to start position. Repeat the movement until you have completed your set.

✦ **TIPS**

Remember to keep your elbows close to your head. Don't lock your elbows at the start position.

✦ **VARIATIONS**

You may perform this exercise in a seated position.

You may perform this exercise one arm at a time, seated or standing.

Standing double-arm overhead triceps
extension, start

Standing double-arm overhead triceps
extension, finish

Triceps Exercise #3
Double-Arm Kickback

The double-arm kickback strengthens, shapes, and tones the entire triceps area, especially the outer head of the muscle.

✦ **POSITION**   Stand with your feet together and bend slightly at the knees and the waist. Hold a dumbbell in each hand, palms facing your body, and bend your elbows so the dumbbells are held in line with your pectoral muscles.

✦ **MOVEMENT**   Keeping your elbows close to your body, extend your arms back until your elbows are locked. (The dumbbells should be just about behind your body.) Return to start position and repeat the movement until you have completed your set.

✦ **TIPS**   Flex (squeeze) your triceps muscle each time you reach the "kicked back" position. Beware of the tendency to let your elbows wander out, away from your body. Keep them close to your waist throughout the exercise.

✦ **VARIATION**   You may perform this exercise one arm at a time.

Summary of Triceps Exercises

PRE-WORKOUT STRETCH
Cross-face triceps extension

TRICEPS ROUTINE
Cross-face triceps extension
Standing double-arm overhead triceps extension
Double-arm kickback

Double-arm kickback, start   **Double-arm kickback, finish**

FLATTENING THE ABDOMINAL AREA

Most women would give just about anything to have a lean waistline. Why is it so difficult to get rid of the excess fat around the abdominal area and to build a girdle of tight, appealing muscles in its place?

Quite simply, the three favorite places for fat accumulation on women are the hips, buttocks, and abdomen—and which area attracts the most on you depends upon your particular genetics.

When trying to lose that last bit of fat, it's always the abdominal area that stubbornly holds its little "paunch," usually below the navel. Even if you're exercising and following our workout, your developing girdle of muscles will be covered over by that layer of fat until you have dieted down to your ideal weight.

If you've severely neglected your abdominal area for years, we don't want to fool you. It will take you six months to a year to achieve a flat, shapely waistline, and in some cases even a bit longer. This is especially true for women over forty, because you may have experienced prolapses of the abdominal area, a condition in which the muscles, because of a lack of exercise, have fallen forward. No amount of dieting can cure this condition. Only proper exercise can help. The good news is, we have seen many women with this condition—forty, fifty, and older—achieve what they once thought was impossible, simply by being persistent and continuing to exercise, and by realizing that it took a long time to get out of shape so it may take a while to get in shape.

If you want to assure yourself of a flat, attractive waistline, you'll have to make a firm commitment to an abdominal workout as well as to a nutritional plan. Exercise will firm your stomach, but it's proper eating that will help you to lose the excess fat there.

You may choose to do some of the extra work recommended in Chapter 4 if you wish to speed up your progress. But even if you don't, if you stick to the basic workout and do it no matter how you feel, refusing to give in to your mood or discouraging thoughts, you'll get the results in time. It's inevitable.

Can an Abdominal Routine Make the Waist Smaller?

Weak muscles are tightened and toned, giving you a flat midsection, by doing the exercises prescribed in this chapter, but nothing short of diet can really remove the fat in order to take inches off the waist. This can be clearly seen in the case of obese women. When an obese woman loses a lot of weight, her waistline is reduced significantly.

Keep in mind that although losing weight usually makes the waist smaller, it is only by exercising properly (as prescribed in this chapter) that you can tighten and tone the waist-abdominal area. In other words, it is possible to have a small waist but a prolapsed midsection that is soft and flabby. In fact, even with liposuction the waist and abdominal area will not be toned. Only exercise can do that.

You must also realize that the waistline is largely determined by genetics. It is the angle at which the external and internal oblique muscles (see muscle description below) slant toward each other that determines the size of the waist. The greater the slant of these muscles, the smaller your waistline will be. There is nothing you can do to change the slant of these muscles. So once you have reached your ideal weight and toned your muscles to the maximum, learn to live with your waistline, whether it's twenty-seven inches or twenty-four! You'll look great either way, because your entire body will be in proportion.

When Exercise and Dieting Are Not Enough

If you have severely stretched skin in the abdominal area due to childbirth or continual weight gain and loss (large amounts of about fifty pounds or more—up and down the scale), you may find that even once you have lost the weight you have loose skin on your abdominal area. Working out with weights can create a firm, muscular structure in the abdominal area that acts as a girdle to help pull your stomach in; however, these muscles will never be big enough to pull taut that severely stretched skin. If you follow this program for a year and find that, although your stomach is firm and toned, you still have loose skin there, you may want to consider a "tummy tuck," or a partial "tummy tuck." These operations can be performed by a qualified cosmetic surgeon.

Some women find, no matter how much they work out or how much they diet, they still have a "little pot" of fat in their lower abdominal area. In order to get rid of this last bit of fat, some women would have to diet down to an anorexic state. If this is your situation you may want to consult a plastic surgeon for possible liposuction.

In the following pages you'll find out not only how to get rid of excess fat, but how to tighten, tone, and beautify your abdominal muscles with sensuous lines of definition. Before you begin your workout, however, it's a good idea to familiarize yourself with the physiology and function of the abdominal muscles.

Muscle Description

The abdominal area consists of four muscle groups: the rectus abdominis, the external obliques, the internal obliques, and the transversus abdominis.

The rectus abdominis is an elongated, segmented muscle attached to the fifth, sixth, and seventh ribs near the breastbone. This extremely long muscle runs along the abdominal wall and is attached on the other end to the pubic bone of the pelvis.

The rectus abdominis functions to pull the torso toward the lower body when sitting up from a lying down position. The crunch, the knee-up, the floor side-bend, and the sit-up with a twist help tighten, strengthen, and define the rectus abdominis.

The external oblique muscles originate at the side of the lower ribs and run diagonally to the rectus abdominis. They are attached to the sheath of fibrous tissue that surrounds the rectus abdominis. These muscles function with other muscles to rotate the trunk and flex the torso.

The internal oblique muscles lie beneath the external obliques and run at right angles to them. It is this angle that forms the shape of the waistline and determines its size. The greater the slant of the oblique muscles, the narrower the waist.

The internal oblique muscles help to keep the waistline area from drooping forward. These muscles also function to twist and turn the torso. Any twisting motion without the use of weights helps tighten and strengthen the oblique muscles.

The transversus abdominis muscles originate on the side

of the abdominal wall and run across the midsection of the abdominal cavity. The transversus muscles function to pull the lower stomach in. The knee-up and the floor side-bend help tighten, tone, and strengthen the transversus abdominis muscles.

Before you begin your abdominal routine it's a good idea to do one general abdominal stretch.

Abdominal Routine

The Circle Stretch

This stretch relaxes the entire abdominal area. It also stretches the chest, shoulder, neck, and lower back muscles.

✦ **POSITION**

Stand with your legs shoulder width apart, and your arms straight up above your head. Let your entire body relax.

✦ **STRETCH**

Slowly bend forward at the waist until your upper body is approximately parallel to the floor. Then without resting, circle around to the right until you feel a full stretch on the left of your waist area. Without resting, circle around to the back and let your torso fall as far as is comfortable. Without resting, circle around to your left side and feel the stretch on the right of your waist area. Circle back around to the front. Continue to circle around until you have completed your stretch.

✦ **TIMING**

Do three to five circles in each direction.

✦ **TIPS**

Let your arms go wherever they may, as you completely relax your body and circle around.

Circle stretch, start

Circle stretch, midpoint

Abdominal Exercise #1
Crunch

〜〜〜〜〜〜〜〜〜〜〜〜〜〜〜〜〜〜〜〜〜〜

The crunch tightens and tones the entire rectus abdominis muscle, with special emphasis on the upper abdominal area. If you do the crunch with a twist, it also helps develop the internal and external oblique muscles.

✦ **POSITION**

Lie flat on your back on the floor and place your legs over an exercise bench so your thighs are perpendicular to the floor. Place your hands behind your head or cross them at your chest.

✦ **MOVEMENT**

With your head slightly forward and your neck locked, curl your torso upward until your shoulders are completely off the floor, continually flexing (squeezing) your upper abdominal muscles as hard as possible. Continue to flex your upper abdominal muscles as you return to start position. Repeat the movement until you have completed your set.

✦ **TIPS**

Do not sit all the way up. Raise only your shoulders off the floor, not your entire back.

Beware of the temptation to rest each time you return to start position.

Keep your movement fluid. Don't give in to the temptation to bounce and jerk.

✦ **VARIATION**

You may perform the "crunch twist" by moving from side to side. Try to touch your left knee with your right elbow and your right knee with your left elbow. Of course, since you're not allowed to lift more than your shoulders off the ground, you will not really be able to do this. The idea is to move from side to side in a mock effort to touch the alternate knee. This movement will help develop the external oblique muscles, which give the waistline a slim appearance.

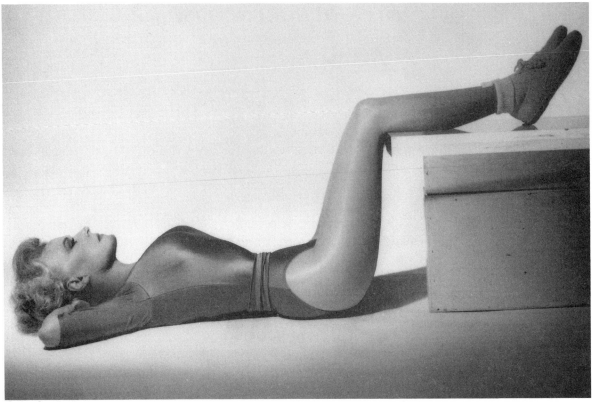

Crunch, start

Crunch, finish

Abdominal Exercise #2
Knee-Up

~~~~~~

The knee-up tightens and tones the entire abdominal wall, with special emphasis on the lower abdominal area, the transversus abdominis.

✦ **POSITION**

Lie on the floor or on a flat exercise bench and extend your legs, ankles together and toes pointed outward, straight out in front of you.

✦ **MOVEMENT**

Bend your legs at the knees and pull them up as close to your chest as possible. At the same time, flex your lower abdominal muscles. Return to start position and repeat the movement until you have completed your set.

✦ **TIPS**

For greater results, hold your legs-to-chest position for three seconds as you flex (squeeze) your lower abdominals as hard as possible.

Beware of the tendency to hold your breath. Remember to breathe naturally.

Keep flexing your lower abdominals throughout the movement—not just on the pulling-in movement, but on the extending movement as well.

✦ **VARIATION**

You may perform this exercise by alternating legs, right-left, right-left, and so on.

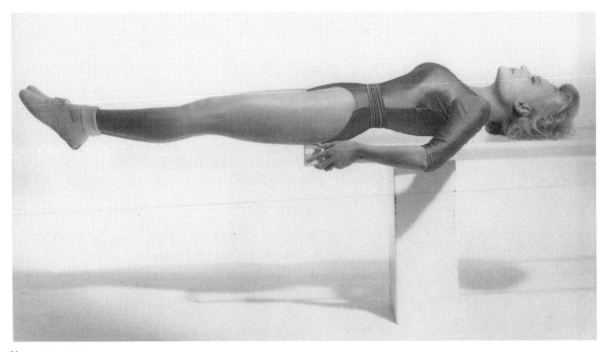

Knee-up, start

Knee-up, finish

Abdominal Exercise #3
Floor Side-Bend

~~~~~~

This exercise tightens, tones, and develops the entire abdominal area (rectus abdominis and transversus abdominis).

✦ **POSITION**

Lie on the floor on your right side, with your body in a perfectly straight line. Keep your knees together and place your right forearm under your head for comfort. Place your left hand on the floor for support.

✦ **MOVEMENT**

Keeping your upper body riveted to the floor and keeping your knees together and legs unbent, raise your legs as high as possible while flexing your entire abdominal area. Repeat the movement until you have completed your set. Perform a set for the other side of your body.

✦ **TIPS**

Remember to apply continual tension to your abdominal area as you work. Keep your body in a straight line. Do not bend your knees.

✦ **VARIATION**

If you have someone to hold down your feet, you may do a reverse side-bend by keeping your waist-to-ankle area riveted to the floor and raising only your torso.

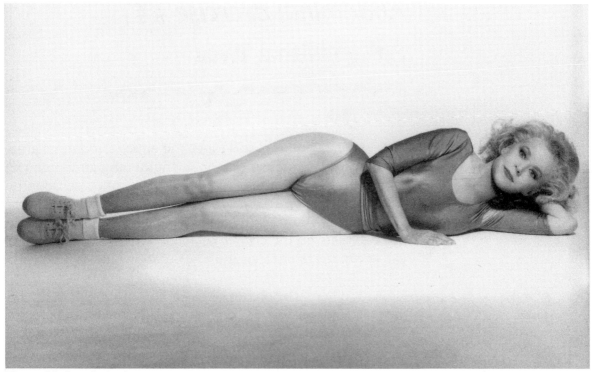

Floor side-bend, start

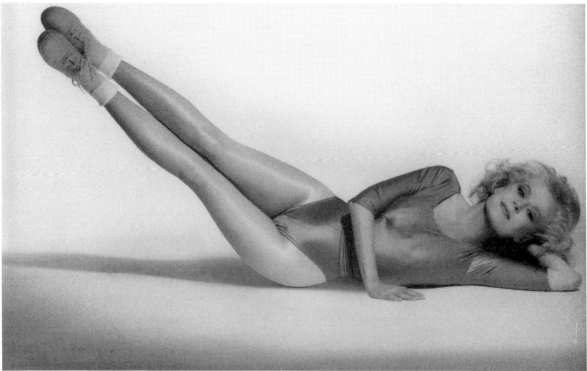

Floor side-bend, finish

Abdominal Exercise #4
Sit-Up with a Twist

〜〜〜〜〜〜〜〜〜〜〜〜〜〜〜〜

This exercise tightens and tones the entire abdominal area. It is an excellent movement for strengthening and toning all major abdominal muscles; however, it cannot be done by all. Check with your doctor to see if your particular physiology allows you to enjoy this movement. If you cannot do this exercise, do the crunch instead, adding the same twist you see in these photographs.

✦ **POSITION**

Lie on the floor, flat on your back with your knees bent and the soles of your feet flat on the floor. Place your hands behind your head.

✦ **MOVEMENT**

Using a fluid movement and flexing your entire abdominal area, rise to a twist-sitting position by twisting your body as you rise, placing your right elbow on your left knee. Return to start and repeat the movement for the other side of your body. Continue this left-right twist movement until you have completed fifteen to twenty-five repetitions for each side of your body.

✦ **TIPS**

Do not allow yourself to fall nearly to start position. Control your movements at all times.

Summary of Abdominal Exercises

PRE-WORKOUT STRETCH
The circle

ABDOMINAL ROUTINE
Crunch
Knee-up
Floor side-bend
Sit-up with a twist

Sit-up with a twist, start

Sit-up with a twist, finish

Note: For additional stomach exercises, see Bibliography for *Gut Busters*.

SHAPING THE CALVES

The calf muscles lend balance and beauty to the leg. There is no way a woman can have perfect legs without also having curvaceous calves. Shapely calves balance out the leg and help create a sensuous, appealing look. Well-developed thigh (quadriceps) muscles cannot stand alone. They must be complemented by well-developed calves.

There are other reasons for developing the calf muscles. Weak calf muscles usually cause foot problems. For those of you who wear high heels it is especially important to exercise the calf muscles, which otherwise may be shortened through abuse.

Another reason to develop the calves is to help correct the look of bowed or slightly bowed legs. While working out with weights cannot straighten bent bone, it *can* help build a muscle that will partially hide bowlegs.

Bowleggedness is due to bone that was soft at one time—usually during childhood. If there was a substantial weight gain at that time, the bone bent. After that, the bone calcified and became hard—the way steel does once heated and allowed to cool. Like cooled steel, the bowed bones in the calf cannot be straightened. They will remain permanently misshaped.

If you follow the workout prescribed in this chapter, you can build a calf muscle that will help hide a misshaped bone, but only if the bone is not severely misshaped.

Before you begin your calf workout you should understand something about the way the calf muscles work.

Muscle Description

The calf muscles consist of two muscle groups: the gastrocnemius and the soleus.

The gastrocnemius is a two-headed muscle that originates at the lower end of the thighbone and is connected to the Achilles tendon of the lower leg in the midcalf area. The gastrocnemius muscle functions to flex the knee and plantarflex the foot (extend it downward).

The soleus muscle originates on the back of the tibia and head of the fibula bones. It lies just underneath the gastrocnemius muscle, but does not pass the knee joint. For this reason, the soleus functions to plantarflex the foot only, not to flex the knee.

The standing calf raise and the seated calf raise help to develop and shape the gastrocnemius and underlying soleus muscles.

Before beginning your full calf routine it's a good idea to do a general calf stretch.

Calf Routine

Achilles Stretch

This stretch loosens and relaxes the Achilles tendon and stretches out the gastrocnemius and soleus muscles. It also helps prevent muscle cramping in the calf area.

◆ **POSITION**

Stand about three feet from a wall or pole with your feet together and your ankles almost touching. Lean forward and touch the wall or grasp the pole with both hands.

◆ **STRETCH**

Bending the elbows and keeping your back straight and feet flat on the ground, lower your body toward the wall until your elbows are touching the wall.

◆ **TIMING**

Perform three three-second stretches.

◆ **TIPS**

It is crucial that you allow enough space between you and the wall to get a good stretch, yet not so much space that you are unable to perform the movement without lifting your heels from the ground.

Keep your mind on your calf muscles as you perform this stretch.

◆ **VARIATION**

You may stretch your calf muscles by placing the soles of your feet on the edge of a stair and lowering your heels as far down as possible.

Calf Exercise #1
Seated Calf Raise

The seated calf raise shapes the gastrocnemius and soleus muscles.

✦ **POSITION**

Sit at the edge of a chair or exercise bench with a weight on top of both knees. Place a thick book under the soles of your feet so that your heels are completely off the book. Lower your heels as far to the floor as possible. You legs should be in an *L* position, your toes pointed straight ahead.

✦ **MOVEMENT**

Raise your heels to the highest possible point and feel the flex in your calf muscles. Lower your heels until you feel a full stretch in your calf muscles. Repeat the movement until you have completed your set.

✦ **TIPS**

Beware of the temptation to merely bounce up and down on your toes. Maintain a fluid movement at all times.

✦ **VARIATIONS**

You may perform this exercise with your toes pointed outward or with your toes pointed inward. Some people do one set in each direction: straight, inward, and outward.

You may perform this exercise on the seated calf machine found in most gyms.

Seated calf raise, start

Seated calf raise, finish

Calf Exercise #2
Standing Calf Raise

The standing calf raise shapes the gastrocnemius and soleus muscles.

✦ **POSITION**

Stand on a thick book with just the balls of your feet on the book. Holding a dumbbell in each hand, lower your heels as far to the ground as possible.

✦ **MOVEMENT**

Raise yourself onto your toes as high as possible. When you reach the highest point, flex your calf muscle as hard as possible. Return to start position and repeat the movement until you have completed your set.

✦ **TIPS**

Be sure to descend to the lowest point when you return to start position and to rise to the highest point on each up movement.

✦ **VARIATIONS**

You may perform this exercise with toes pointed inward or toes pointed outward.

You may do a stair calf raise by performing the exercise at the edge of a stair.

If you are unable to maintain balance without holding on to something, you may perform this movement one leg at a time, as pictured in the "variation" photograph.

Summary of Calf Exercises

PRE-WORKOUT STRETCH

Achilles

CALF ROUTINE

Seated calf raise
Standing calf raise

Standing calf raise, start   **Standing calf raise, finish**   **One-legged calf raise (Variation)**

PART III:
Workout Day Two—
Thighs, Hips and
Buttocks, Back,
and Biceps

The thighs are the bane of many women. "If I could only shape and slim down these thighs," they say. But what they don't realize is, the last thing a woman—especially an older woman—really wants to do is diet to the point of emaciation to "get rid" of her oversize thighs. What she really wants to do is get rid of the excess fat on the thigh and build a firm, strong, shapely muscle there, so when she does lose the excess weight she doesn't look like a thin older woman with atrophying muscles.

When you develop some shapely muscles on the front of your thigh, your thigh will not look fat. It will take on a tight, toned, youthful look. Also, a little development on the back of your thigh will not detract from your appearance, but rather will enhance it. Instead of cellulite you'll have a smooth, curvaceous hamstring (assuming, of course, that you also follow the balanced-nutrition eating plan presented in Chapter 5).

Thigh muscles don't just begin to disintegrate automatically. Atrophy occurs as the result of wrong dieting, disuse and immobilization, or neuromuscular disease.

WHAT HAPPENED TO YOUR THIGHS?

If you've ever gone on a starvation diet, chances are you've done some damage to all your muscles. But since the thigh muscles are quite large, chances are you've done a fair share of the damage there. Your thighs have literally been "eaten away" for survival purposes. Here's what may have happened.

Unlike the protein found in nervous and connective tissues, muscle and liver tissue can be eaten away during starvation periods. When you go on a severe calorie-restricted diet, the body begins to consume stored energy and protein found in the muscle in order to survive. When this happens, the individual muscle cells lose their contractile protein and myoglobin content. The end result is an atrophied muscle.

The other common reason for muscle atrophy is disuse. Unfortunately, as people get older they often exercise less—when they actually need to exercise more. (As mentioned before, we lose a fraction of overall body muscle every year after thirty, and we need to work out just to replace that muscle.) As it turns out, the old adage is true: "Use it or lose it."

Resistance Exercises Reverse Muscle Atrophy

The wonderful news is, you can restore atrophied muscles. Numerous studies have proved that muscles do respond to exercise (unless one has a specific neuromuscular disease). This fact can be demonstrated by physical therapy, which works with specific atrophied muscles for restoration. Physical therapists are, in fact, able to reverse muscle atrophy in patients who are completely immobile. These patients are unable to exercise actively, even with "passive exercise," where the physical therapist moves and exercises the atrophied body part to restore diminished muscles. How much more does exercise work when you actively participate by moving your own body part to restore atrophied muscle? A lot more.

The resistance exercises found in this chapter can restore atrophied thigh muscles and give them shape and beauty once again. Here's how it works physiologically. Working out with weights increases the size of the muscle cells and their cellular components. As the cells enlarge, greater amounts of contractile protein, myoglobin, and glycogen are stored in the muscle. Nutrients and wastes are delivered to and from the muscle cells more efficiently. The overall muscle becomes healthy and begins to be restored in size and strength. The end result is complete reversal of atrophy and the development of brand new muscle tissue.

So, if you work out with weights the right way, you can indeed say that you are not getting older, you are in fact (at least in the muscles you create) getting "newer." Think about that!

Before we discuss the details on how to tighten, tone, shape, and strengthen your thigh muscles, it's a good idea to become acquainted with the physiology and function of the thigh muscles.

Muscle Description

There are four groups of thigh muscles: the sartorius, the adductors, the quadriceps femoris, and the hamstrings.

The sartorius muscle runs across the thigh, from the hip-bone to the inside of the knee. It is the longest muscle in the human body and functions to rotate the thigh. This muscle is challenged by the sissy squat.

The adductor muscles are located on the inside of the thigh. The largest and most important of these muscles is the adductor magnus.

The adductor muscles originate from the lower pelvic area on the pubis (pubic bone) and insert on the shaft of the thighbone. In cooperation with other inner thigh muscles, they work to flex, rotate, and pull the legs together from a spread-apart stance. The sissy squat strengthens and develops the adductor muscles.

The quadriceps femoris (commonly known as the quadriceps) consists of four muscles that travel along the front of the thigh and end at the kneecap. The four muscles are the rectus femoris, which originates on the front of the hip-bone, and the vasti (three muscles grouped together: the vastus lateralis, the vastus medialis, and the vastus intermedius), which originate on the thighbone.

The entire quadriceps group works to extend the leg. The dumbbell lunge, the dumbbell squat, and the sissy squat work to strengthen and develop the quadriceps femoris.

The hamstring muscle group, located on the back of the thigh, consists of three muscles: the biceps femoris (a two-headed muscle) and the semimembranosus and semitendinosus. All three muscles originate in the bony area of the pelvis and end along the back of the knee joint. The hamstring muscle group works to bend the knee.

Be Patient—The Fat Might Be Hindering Your Progress

The thigh muscles are a favorite place for fat accumulation. For this reason, once you start working out you may not see progress until you have followed the balanced nutrition plan and lost the excess fat. Be patient. In a matter of months everything will begin to materialize. In the meantime, don't become discouraged. Most things that are lasting take time to develop!

The Adductor Muscles—A Special Case

As mentioned above, the adductor muscles are located on the inner thigh. While underdeveloped adductor muscles can cause the look of "knock-knees," overdeveloped adductor muscles can cause the thigh to have a "chunky" appearance. For this reason we recommend the following no-weight strengthening exercise for the adductors, rather than one with weights.

Adductor Squeeze

Lie on your side, keeping your entire body in a straight line. Place the foot of your upper leg on the edge of a chair. Keeping that upper leg firmly rooted to the chair, flex the inner thigh of your lower leg as hard as possible, raising that leg until your foot touches the bottom of the chair. Repeat the movement ten times and perform the movement for the other leg. Repeat this set three times for each leg.

Now you are ready to begin your regular thigh workout. Before you begin your thigh routine it's a good idea to do a general thigh stretch.

Thigh Routine

The Quadriceps Stretch

This stretch loosens and limbers the entire quadriceps muscle.

◆ POSITION

Lie on the floor on your left side, with your left arm extended straight up, left ear leaning on your left biceps muscle.

◆ STRETCH

Curl your right leg behind you by flexing your right knee until you can grasp your right ankle with your right hand.

Pull your ankle back until you feel a full stretch in your quadriceps muscle. Repeat the stretch for the other leg.

✦ TIMING   Perform three ten-to-fifteen-second stretches for each leg.

✦ TIPS   Keep your mind on your quadriceps muscle as you perform the stretch.

Thigh Exercise #1
Dumbbell Squat

~~~~~~

The squat works to tighten and tone the quadriceps muscle. In addition, it firms the hip and buttocks area.

✦ **POSITION**

Stand with your feet a natural width apart and your arms straight down at your sides, with a dumbbell in each hand, palms facing your sides. (You will not use the dumbbells until you have "broken in gently," as described earlier.)

✦ **MOVEMENT**

Without leaning forward, looking straight ahead, bend at the knees and lower your body until your upper thighs are parallel to the floor. (If you can't go down that low, go as far as you can without straining your knees.) Feel the stretch in your quadriceps muscle. Return to start position and flex (squeeze) your quadriceps muscles. Repeat the movement until you have completed your set.

✦ **TIPS**

You may place a two-by-four piece of wood under your heels for balance.

The harder you flex your quadriceps on the return movement, the firmer your thighs will be.

Don't merely drop down and bounce up. Control your movements. Keep your mind on your quadriceps throughout the exercise.

✦ **VARIATION**

You may perform this exercise with a barbell placed on your shoulders.

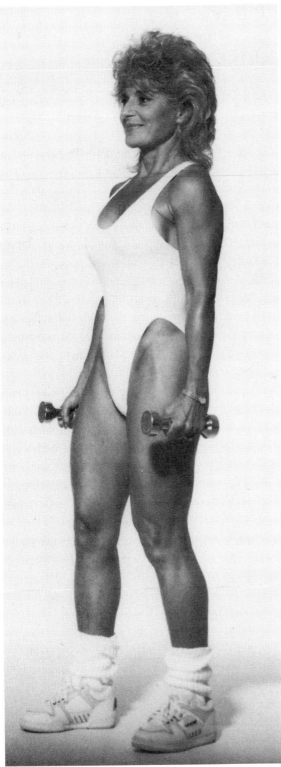

Dumbbell squat, start

Dumbbell squat, finish

Thigh Exercise #2
Dumbbell Lunge

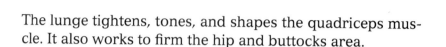

The lunge tightens, tones, and shapes the quadriceps muscle. It also works to firm the hip and buttocks area.

✦ **POSITION**

Stand in a natural position with your arms straight down at your sides and a dumbbell in each hand, palms facing your sides. (You will not use the dumbbells until you have "broken in gently," as described earlier.)

✦ **MOVEMENT**

With your right foot, step forward about two to three feet and bend your right knee as you lunge forward as far as possible. Return to start position and repeat the movement for the other leg. Repeat the alternate-leg lunging until you have completed your set.

✦ **TIPS**

Be sure you can feel the stretch in your quadriceps muscle as you lunge. If you can't, perhaps you're not lunging far enough forward. If you look straight ahead, you'll find it easier to maintain balance. (It may take a few weeks before you stop careening. This is normal.) Beware of the tendency to bounce off your leg when rising from the lunge position.

✦ **VARIATION**

You may do this exercise with a barbell placed across your shoulders.

Dumbbell lunge, start

Dumbbell lunge, finish

Thigh Exercise #3
Sissy Squat

The sissy squat tightens and tones the quadriceps, sartoris, and adductor muscles, and is the most effective exercise for defining the front of the thigh.

◆ **POSITION**

Stand near a table or bar for balance, with your feet about eight inches apart.

◆ **MOVEMENT**

Raise your body up by leaning backward as you rise up on your toes. Continue to lean back until your body is at a forty-five-degree angle with the floor. Thrust your hips and knees as far forward as possible (to the point where your hips are in line with your ankles). Return to start position and repeat the movement until you have completed your set.

◆ **TIPS**

Be sure to feel a complete stretch in your quadriceps muscles as they are fully elongated. Don't despair if you can't bend the full forty-five-degree-angle position. Bend as far as you can. In time you may be able to go farther.

◆ **VARIATION**

You may perform this exercise lying on a leg-press machine. Lie flat on your back and perform the same hip-thrusting, thigh-stretching movement from this position.

Summary of Thigh Exercises

STRENGTHENING EXERCISE FOR INNER THIGH (ADDUCTORS)

Adductor squeeze

PRE-WORKOUT STRETCH

Quadriceps

THIGH ROUTINE

Dumbbell squat
Dumbbell lunge
Sissy squat

Sissy squat, start

Sissy squat, finish

TRIMMING THE HIPS AND BUTTOCKS

The hips and buttocks have always been an embarrassment to most women. For some reason fat seems to gravitate to this area. That reason is not really a mystery. Even a trim woman will carry up to eight pounds of adipose tissue in the hip and buttocks area, eight pounds more than an equally trim man. Why is this so?

The answer is simple. Women have been given this "boon" to protect them from injury during childbearing. For the same reason, a woman's pelvis is usually broader than a man's. Because of nature's endowment, it is most difficult to trim and tone the hip and buttocks area to the ideal shape we have in mind. However, there's a lot that can be done. If, however, your goal is to achieve extremely narrow hips, or buttocks completely free of fat, you will not achieve it, even if you become anorexic. What you can do, by following this workout, is tighten, strengthen, and tone your hip and buttocks area to the point where you feel good about yourself.

You may have noticed that your once high, firm buttocks are somewhat saggy now. This is the normal process of time. But with resistance training, as prescribed in this chapter, you can begin to reverse the effects of sagging, even in your forties, fifties, and older. Just like all other muscles in the body, the gluteal muscles respond to specific exercises.

Keep in mind, however, that all the exercise in the world won't make your buttocks smaller if you continue to overeat. As we mentioned earlier, the three favorite places for excess fat storage on women are the abdominals, thighs, and the hip and buttocks area. But if you trim down to your ideal body weight, you can be sure that the size of your buttocks will be significantly reduced.

In addition, if you've been carrying a heavy load of adipose tissue on your buttocks, the force of gravity will have pulled the buttocks muscles down because of the added weight. The bigger your buttocks, the stronger the pull of gravity. So even if you get the weight off you'll still notice the sag. Once again, that's why dieting and resistance training go hand in hand.

But let's not go overboard. There's no need for you to completely hone down your buttocks. The fact is, believe it or not, women do look better with curves than with straight lines. So even if you still think your buttocks are too big or your hips are too large, once you have reached the tight, toned stage, give yourself a break. You're probably the only one who feels that way about you. Even other women are not judging you as harshly as you're judging yourself.

Vanity is not the only reason to exercise your hip and buttocks area. It is important to have strong hip muscles and bones as you get older, in order to prevent fractures. Proper exercise will not only assure you of stronger, less brittle bones, it will increase your flexibility.

Muscle Description

The hip and buttocks area consists of two muscle groups: the gluteal muscles and the lateral outward rotators.

The gluteal muscle group consists of three muscles: the gluteus maximus, the gluteus medius, and the gluteus minimus. The largest of the gluteal muscles, the gluteus maximus, originates from the iliac crest of the hipbone and runs down to the thighbone. This muscle works to extend and rotate the thigh when extreme force is needed, such as in stair-climbing or running. The gluteus medius is placed just under the gluteus maximus. It functions to raise the leg out to the side and to keep the hips even when you shift your weight from one leg to the other. The gluteus minimis is located just in front of the gluteus medius and functions in the same manner.

The side leg lift, the kneeling kickback, and the hip raise all work to tighten and strengthen the entire gluteus muscle group.

The lateral outward rotators consist of six small muscles that originate under the gluteus maximus and are attached to the thighbone. They function to extend the thigh and rotate the hip joint. The side leg lift and the hip raise help strengthen the lateral outward rotators.

Stretching the Hip Area

Before you attempt to strengthen and develop the muscles of your hip and buttocks area, it's a good idea to stretch the ligaments of the hip joints. Here are three simple stretches that will help you accomplish that goal. Doing them will help increase the range of your hip ligaments and in turn make you less prone to injury. Of course, the next step will be to strengthen the hip and buttocks area. First the stretches.

The Inner Hip Stretch

Stand with your hands on your waist and your feet two and a half feet apart. Keep your right foot on the floor and shift your weight to your left foot. Without moving your right foot, lower yourself to a squatting position with your weight on your left leg, until you feel a full stretch in your inner hip. Keeping your mind on your inner hip area, hold the position for five seconds and repeat the movement for your other leg.

The Front Hip Stretch

Place your hands, arms extended straight out in front of you, on a desk or table, and put one leg three feet behind you as you bend the leg closest to your hands. Keeping your arms straight, slowly drop your pelvic girdle down and in, until you feel a full stretch in the front part of your hip joint. Be sure to keep your trunk in an upright position throughout the exercise. Keeping your mind on your front hip area, hold the position for ten to fifteen seconds.

The Outer Hip Stretch

Holding on to a stationary object such as a door jamb, assume a side-facing position. Place your feet hip width apart and balance yourself so your weight is evenly distributed. Shift your weight to your outer leg and continue to shift it until your hips are over the leg (so your body depicts the letter *C*). Keep your shoulders in place. Keeping your mind on your outer hip area, hold the position for ten to fifteen seconds. Repeat the movement for the other side of your body.

Strengthening Weak Hips

Before you begin your regular hips and buttocks exercises, which will tighten, tone, and lift your buttocks, it is necessary to strengthen the ligaments, tendons, and bones of the area. The following preconditioning exercises will help you gain flexibility and strength. Here's how it works.

When you perform a given exercise, the tendons and muscles pull as you contract your muscles. The body goes into a survival mode. It causes the bones to become stronger in order to cope with the work. By doing specific exercises for the hips and buttocks, you will be giving yourself an insurance policy against future injury—especially to the hip joints.

Unless you've been exercising your hip and buttocks area for some time and feel that you've already developed ligament, tendon, and bone strength, it's a good idea to do the following pre-strengthening exercises before you begin your regular hips and buttocks routine.

Hip Flexor and Extensor

Stand with your feet shoulder width apart and shift your weight onto your right leg. Raise your left knee until your thigh is parallel to the floor. Return to start position and repeat the movement three times. Repeat the movement for the other leg.

Hip Abductor

Lie on the floor on your side, with your body in a straight line. Raise your upper leg as high as possible, while keeping your toes pointed forward. Return to start position and re-peat the movement three times. Repeat the movement for the other leg.

Now you are ready to do your regular hips and buttocks exercises. Before you begin to work out, however, it's a good idea to do one general hips and buttocks stretch.

Hips and Buttocks Routine

Bent-Knee Bottom Pull Stretch

This stretch elongates and relaxes the entire hip and but-tocks area.

✦ **POSITION**

Lie flat on your back on the floor and bend your right leg, keeping your right foot flat on the floor. Bend your left knee and place your hands around your left leg along the calf and shin bone. Curl your fingers around your leg.

✦ **STRETCH**

Pull your left leg gently toward your chest until you feel a full stretch in your left hip and buttocks area. Perform the stretch for the other side of your body.

✦ **TIMING**

Perform three ten- to fifteen-second stretches for each leg.

✦ **TIPS**

Keep your head and lower back flat on the floor as you stretch. Flex your abdominal muscles. This will help you reap the full benefit of the stretch.

Hips and Buttocks Exercise #1
Side Leg Lift

The side leg lift tightens, tones, and shapes the entire hip and buttocks area.

◆ **POSITION**

Lie on the floor on your right side, supporting yourself with your right elbow. Pin your right leg to the floor as you prepare to lift your left leg.

◆ **MOVEMENT**

Lift your left leg as high as you can and flex your left buttock as hard as possible. Continue to squeeze your left buttock as you lower your left leg to start position. Repeat the movement until you've completed your set. Repeat the set for your right leg.

◆ **TIPS**

Keep your working leg in a straight line with the leg that's "riveted" to the floor, knee and toes pointed forward. Continually flex (squeeze) your working buttock muscle.

◆ **VARIATION**

You may work both legs at the same time if you sit on the floor, placing your hands under your buttocks (so you can feel the "squeeze" of your buttocks) and open and close your legs in a scissorlike movement. Be sure to go as wide as possible.

Side leg lift, start

Side leg lift, finish

Hips and Buttocks Exercise #2
Kneeling Kickback

The kneeling kickback tightens and tones the entire hip and buttocks area. It also strengthens the lower back.

✦ **POSITION**

Kneel on your hands and knees, and thrust the weight of your body onto your right knee. Lift your left knee until your midthigh is touching your chest. Your back will be in a curved or rounded position.

✦ **MOVEMENT**

Push your left leg out behind you until it is parallel to the floor. Without stopping, continue to move your leg upward as high as you can, squeezing your left buttock as hard as possible. Your foot should be extended back and your toes pointed as far back as possible. Return to start position and repeat the movement until you have completed your set. Repeat the set for the right leg.

✦ **TIPS**

As you reach the high position, flex (squeeze) your working buttock as hard as possible.

If you have back trouble, do not lift your leg higher than parallel to the floor. This will prevent hyperextension of the back.

✦ **VARIATION**

You may start with your leg extended straight out behind you in the parallel to the floor position and do the entire exercise from that stance.

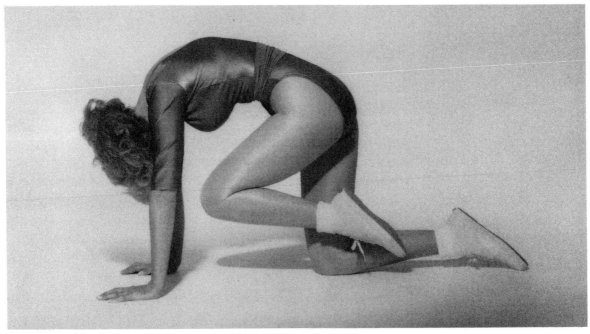

Kneeling kickback, start

Kneeling kickback, finish

Hips and Buttocks Exercise #3
Hip Raise

~~~~~~

The hip raise tightens and tones the entire hip and buttocks area and strengthens the lower back as well.

✦ **POSITION**

Lie flat on your back. Bend your knees until the soles of your feet are flat on the floor. Keep your hands at your sides, ready to check your working hip and buttocks area for maximum flex.

✦ **MOVEMENT**

Raise your hips and buttocks off the floor and at the same time flex (squeeze) that area as hard as possible. As you raise yourself, place your fingers on each buttock to see how hard you're squeezing. Once your entire buttocks is off the floor, flex extra hard for a split second and return to start. Without resting, repeat the movement until you have completed your set.

✦ **TIPS**

What makes this exercise work is the continual flexing of your buttocks muscles.

If you experience pain in your lower back, do the variation instead.

✦ **VARIATION**

You may do this exercise standing. Stand in a natural position and thrust your hips forward, squeezing your buttocks muscles as hard as possible as you thrust. You may place your fingers on your working buttocks to check.

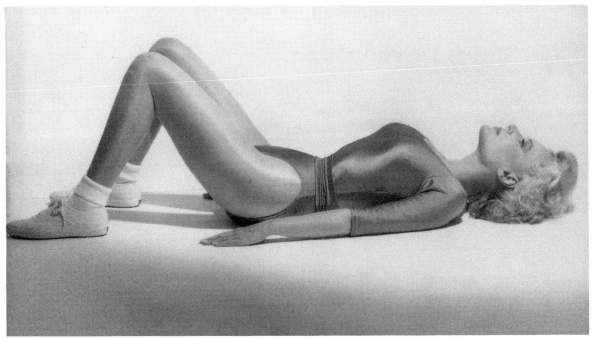

Hip raise, start

Hip raise, finish

Hips and Buttocks Exercise #4
Seated Scissors

The seated scissors tightens and tones the entire hip and buttocks area.

✦ **POSITION**

Sit at the edge of an exercise bench or chair. Holding on to the sides, extend your legs straight out in front of you.

✦ **MOVEMENT**

Without bending your knees, raise your legs up and down in a scissorlike motion, flexing your gluteus maximus (buttocks) muscles as hard as possible. Continue this movement until you have completed your set.

✦ **TIPS**

Be sure to apply continual tension to your buttocks muscles as you work. If you fail to flex your gluteus maximus while working, the exercise will have no effect.

✦ **VARIATIONS**

You may scissor your legs apart and together. You may perform the exercise with light ankle weights (one to three pounds each).

Seated scissors

Hips and Buttocks Exercise #5
Lying Scissors

The lying scissors tightens and tones the entire hip and buttocks area. It also helps tone the inner thigh.

◆ **POSITION**

Lie flat on your back and extend your legs straight up in the air. Do not bend your knees. Extend your arms straight out at your sides for support.

◆ **MOVEMENT**

While flexing your buttocks muscles as hard as possible, extend your legs apart as far as you can, and without resting, return to the legs-together position. Repeat the movement until you have completed your set.

◆ **TIPS**

Beware of the temptation to bend your knees. Keep them straight and keep the pressure on your gluteus maximus muscles.

◆ **VARIATIONS**

You may perform this movement by scissoring your legs up and down. You may perform this movement with light ankle weights (one to three pounds).

Summary of Hips and Buttocks Exercises

HIP STRETCHES

The inner hip stretch
The front hip stretch
The outer hip stretch

PRE-STRENGTHENING EXERCISES

Hip flexor and extensor
Hip abductor

PRE-WORKOUT STRETCH

Bent-knee bottom pull

HIPS AND BUTTOCKS ROUTINE

Side leg lift
Kneeling kickback
Hip raise
Seated scissors
Lying scissors

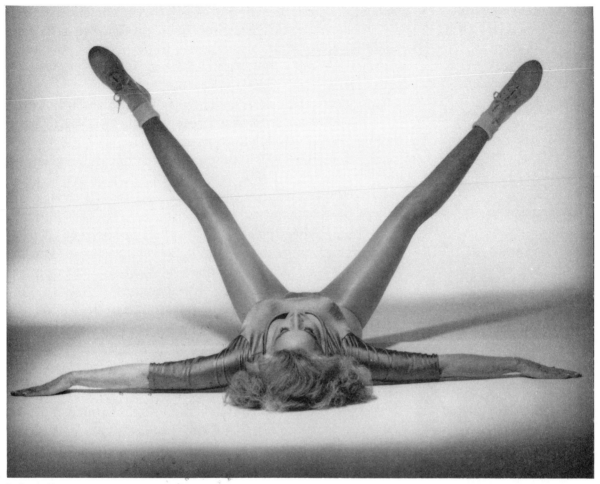

Lying scissors

STRENGTHENING AND BEAUTIFYING THE BACK

It is impossible to overemphasize the importance of exercising the back muscles. Clearly, if you have a weak back you'll be unwilling and/or unable to do most of your other exercises. What's more, a "bad back" will limit all of your activities, not just your workout.

This section will show you how to stretch and strengthen your back so you may ease present back troubles or avoid them in the future. In addition, and perhaps equally important, this section will show you how to develop a beautiful back.

Just what is a beautiful back? It's a well-shaped back, one that has the look of a *V* as opposed to a curved, hunched look. It has pretty lines of definition, as opposed to layers of fat, running along the shoulder blade area. It sends out a message: "I am young and filled with vitality," as opposed to, "I am withered and filled with weakness."

So for the purposes of good health, strength, and beauty, it behooves you to exercise your back. Before you do that, however, it is necessary to get a general idea of where your specific back muscles are located and how they function.

Muscle Description

There are five groups of back muscles that concern us: the erector spinae, the trapezius, the rhomboids (major and minor), the teres (major and minor), and the latissimus dorsi.

The erector spinae consists of interacting muscles located on either side of the spinal column. These muscles form two strong supporting columns that run the length of the back. The erector spinae muscles allow the lower back to bend sideways, to bend backward, and to rotate. If an individual has underdeveloped abdominal muscles, the erector spinae becomes shortened and stiffened. When this happens, the lower back sometimes develops an increased inward curve, which in turn causes pressure on the intervertebral disk in that location. In fact, it is exactly this problem that causes much low back pain.

The stretches and pre-strengthening back exercises in this section will help develop this muscle group. (In addition, of course, you must do your abdominal exercises as explained earlier in this chapter.)

The trapezius is a triangular muscle that originates in the back of the neck at the collarbone and runs to the middle of the back. The upper area of the trapezius muscle functions to shrug the shoulders and pull the head back, while the lower part of the muscle helps stabilize the shoulder blade and pull it down when the arm is raised.

An underdeveloped trapezius muscle causes the neck and shoulder area to appear asymmetrical and even "scrawny," giving a look of age rather than youth. It's important to develop the trapezius muscle in order to balance out the look of the chest-shoulder-neck area. The bent dumbbell row and the seated back lateral help develop and strengthen the trapezius muscle.

The rhomboid muscles originate on the lower cervical vertebrae of the upper spinal column and travel along in an oblique path, inserting between the shoulder blade and the spinal column. The rhomboid major, the larger portion of the muscle, is located directly beneath the rhomboid minor. The rhomboid muscles function to pull the shoulders back and rotate the shoulder blade downward as the arm is lowered and raised.

The rhomboid muscles are developed and strengthened by the bent dumbbell row, the seated back lateral, and the one-arm dumbbell bent row.

The teres muscles originate at the lower portion of the shoulder blade and insert in the upper arm bone. The teres major inserts on the front of the bone, while the teres minor inserts on the back of the bone. These muscles work to rotate the arm and pull it toward the body. The teres muscles are developed and strengthened by the bent dumbbell row, the seated back lateral, and the one-arm dumbbell bent row.

The latissimus dorsi is perhaps the most well known of the back muscle groups, because it is the most visible. The latissimus dorsi gives the back its shape. Well-developed "lats" cause the back to have the shape of a *V* and also help the waist appear smaller.

The latissimus dorsi muscles originate along the spinal column in the middle of the back and travel upward and sideways to the shoulder, inserting in the front of the upper arm. They work to pull the shoulder back and down, and to pull the arm back toward the body. They also work to stabilize the shoulder joints.

The bent dumbbell row develops and strengthens the latissimus dorsi muscles.

How to Strengthen and Beautify Your Back Muscles

The back muscles become weak not so much because of advancing age, but because of disuse. As discussed before, every year after thirty all of the muscles atrophy to a certain extent. However, if you exercise those muscles, the attrition process can be more than compensated for. In fact, if you follow the suggestions outlined in this section, you can have a stronger, younger, healthier back than you had ten years ago!

The best way to cure back problems is to prevent them in the first place. "What?" you say. "I already have back troubles." This may be true. But if you begin an intelligent strengthening program now, you will not only improve the present condition of your back, you will also prevent major future problems.

If you have a weak back the best thing to do is work toward strength and health in stages: Stretch your spine first, then do some pre-strengthening exercises. Then you will be ready for a full strength and beauty back routine.

Stretching the Spine

Although delicately constructed, under normal conditions the spine can withstand a lot of abuse. It's only when the spine becomes inflexible that trouble begins. Your first goal then will be to make your spine more flexible. Here's how.

Exercise your back so the vertebrae are kept apart and blood can circulate throughout them. In order to keep your vertebrae apart and your intervertebral disks healthy, do the following stretches. Be sure to keep your mind focused on your spine as you stretch.

Knee to Chest

Lie flat on your back with your arms alongside your body. Bend your right leg and using both hands, without jerking, pull your knee as close to your chest as possible. Hold the position for ten to fifteen seconds. Repeat the movement for your left leg.

The Hang

If you can find a high bar to hang from, this stretch is great. Grip the bar with both hands and let your body fall into the relaxed "hang" position. Without lurching, slowly move your hips in each direction. Do this for about ten to fifteen seconds.

Reverse Trunk Twist

Lie on the floor, flat on your back, with straight arms at forty-five-degree angles from your body and palms flat against the floor. Bending at the knees, bring your thighs up until they're perpendicular to your trunk. Keeping your knees together, without jerking, move your bent legs to either side, keeping your shoulders on the floor. Repeat three times.

Side Bend

Stand up straight and raise your arms straight up, clasping your hands over the center of your head. Without lurching, slowly bend to the right side, leaning as far as you can, keeping your hands clasped and your arms straight. Feel the stretch in your spine. Repeat the movement for the other side. Repeat the movement three times.

Strengthening the Neglected Back

If you have a weak back, before you begin the regular back workout you should first do the following pre-strengthening exercises.

Pelvic Thrust

Lie flat on your back with your knees bent and your feet flat on the floor. Keep your arms vertical to your body, and raise your pelvic girdle as high as possible. Hold the position for ten to fifteen seconds and repeat the movement three times.

Cross-Body Lift

Get into an all-fours position. Raise your right arm and your left leg, simultaneously, until they are straight out and level with the ground. Don't let your hips rotate, and don't drop the shoulder on the supporting side. Hold this position for ten to fifteen seconds and return to start position. Repeat the movement for the other limbs. Repeat the set three times.

Now you're ready to do your regular back exercises. Before you start, it's a good idea to do one general back stretch.

Back Routine

Bent-Knee Back Stretch

This stretch relaxes the entire upper, middle, and lower back area. It also stretches the shoulders and waist.

✦ POSITION

Stand with your feet about six inches wider than shoulder width apart, knees bent slightly and toes turned out slightly.

✦ STRETCH

Place your right hand on your right thigh, about eight inches above your knee, fingers facing your inner thigh for support. Reach toward your right side with your left arm stretched forward across your body, bending at the waist and stretching your left upper, middle, and lower back muscles in the process. Hold for ten to fifteen seconds and repeat the stretch for the right side of your body.

✦ TIMING

Perform three stretches for each side of your body.

Back Exercise #1
Bent Dumbbell Row

~~~~~~~~~~~~~~~~~~~~~~~~~~~~~~~~

The bent dumbbell row strengthens, shapes, and defines the latissimus dorsi, the trapezius, the rhomboids, and the teres. The rear deltoid and the forearm are worked too.

✦ **POSITION**

Stand with your feet a natural width apart, a dumbbell in each hand, palms facing your body. Bend at the knees and lean forward until your torso is parallel to the floor. With your arms straight down, hold the dumbbells, touching each other, centered in front of your body.

✦ **MOVEMENT**

Raise the dumbbells up until they reach waist height, flexing (squeezing) your latissimus dorsi muscles as you go. Lower the dumbbells to start position and feel a full stretch in your back muscles. Repeat the movement until you have completed your set.

✦ **TIPS**

Keep the torso parallel to the floor at all times.

If you're doing this exercise in front of a mirror, you may look at yourself by bending your neck upward (but be sure to keep your position).

✦ **VARIATION**

You may perform this exercise with a barbell.

Bent dumbbell row, start

Bent dumbbell row, finish

Back Exercise #2
Seated Back Lateral

The seated back lateral strengthens, shapes, and defines the rhomboids, teres, and trapezius muscles.

✦ **POSITION**

Sit at the edge of an exercise bench with a dumbbell in each hand, palms facing your body. Lean forward until your chest is touching your knees. Keep your feet together and let the end of each dumbbell touch your ankles.

✦ **MOVEMENT**

Raise the dumbbells up and back until they reach hip level, rotating the dumbbells as you move so palms are facing forward at the hip-level position. Return to start position and allow the dumbbells to stretch out your back. Repeat the movement until you have completed your set.

✦ **TIPS**

Be sure to flex (squeeze) your upper back muscles. Try squeezing your shoulders together as if you were trying to grip a pencil in the center of your back.

Perform this exercise slowly and with full concentration.

✦ **VARIATION**

You may perform this exercise on any gym back lateral machine.

Seated back lateral, start

Seated back lateral, finish

Back Exercise #3

One-Arm Dumbbell Bent Row

The one-arm dumbbell bent row strengthens, shapes, and defines the rhomboids, teres, and latissimus dorsi muscles. This movement also exercises the biceps muscle.

◆ **POSITION**

Place one hand on your waist and hold a dumbbell in the other hand, palm facing your body. Bend at the waist and knees, and place your feet in a comfortable position.

◆ **MOVEMENT**

Raise your arm to waist level. Keep your arms close to your body and raise your elbow as high as possible. Return to start position and feel a full stretch in your back. Repeat the movement until you've completed your set. Repeat the set for the other arm.

◆ **TIPS**

Do not jerk the dumbbell up or let it drop to start position. Be deliberate in your movements.

◆ **VARIATION**

You may perform this exercise by bending over and holding on to something with one hand.

Summary of Back Exercises

SPINAL STRETCHES

Knee to chest
The hang
Reverse trunk twist
Side bend

STRENGTHENING EXERCISES

Pelvic thrust
Cross-body lift

PRE-WORKOUT STRETCH

Bent-knee back

BACK ROUTINE

Bent dumbbell row
Seated back lateral
One-arm dumbbell bent row

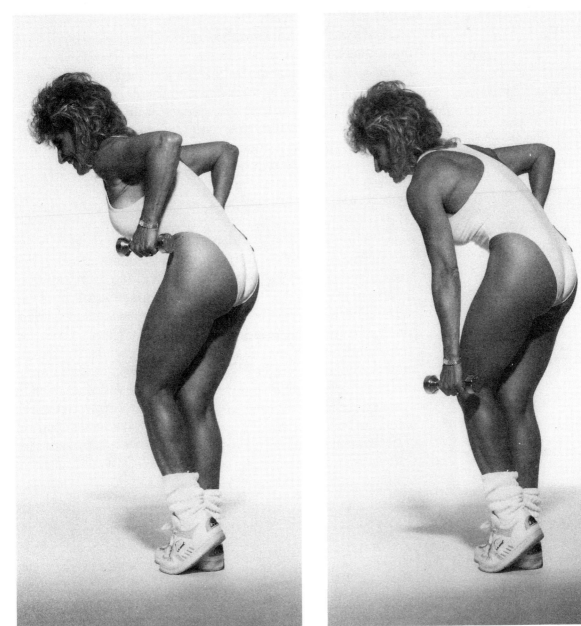

One-arm dumbbell bent row, start

One-arm dumbbell bent row, finish

BALANCING THE BICEPS

The biceps together with the triceps form the upper arm. If you extend your arm straight out to your side, parallel to the floor, palm upward, you can see your biceps. It is the upper side of your arm. But in this position you can't get a full view, because the muscle isn't flexed. Now make a fist and bend your arms at the elbow until your fist nearly touches your shoulder. Now you can see your biceps muscle—if you *can* see it at all! If you can't, you will in a couple of months, and that will be a good thing. Why?

The biceps muscle gives shape and beauty to a woman's arm. A well-shaped biceps speaks of youth and vitality, whereas a flat, atrophied biceps, replaced by fat and sagging skin, speaks of deterioration and advancing age. There's no way around it. If you want to achieve the overall look of a healthy, well-proportioned woman, you can't afford to neglect the exercise of your biceps muscle.

The biceps has traditionally been the muscle used by men when asked to "make a muscle." But don't worry. As you follow our workout you won't develop big, bulky biceps muscles. Instead, you'll create curvaceous, sensuous muscles that give the arm shape and balance. In addition, you'll make that muscle stronger so day-to-day lifting activities are no longer a burden. You'll find you have less strain on your arms in general and you feel stronger. In short, by developing a petite, shapely biceps muscle you will also be building an insurance policy against arm injury.

Muscle Description

The biceps actually consists of two muscle groups: the biceps and the brachialis.

The biceps is a two-headed muscle. One head is short, the other long. Both heads originate on the cavity of the shoulder blade where the upper arm bone inserts into the shoulder. The two heads join to form a raised "hump" about one third down the arm. The other end of the biceps muscle is attached to the bones of the forearm by one connecting tendon.

The brachialis muscle lies just under the biceps, attached to the lower front half of the humerus and the upper end of the forearm.

Both the biceps and the brachialis muscles work to supinate (or twist upward) the hand and flex the arm. The standing alternate hammer curl and the concentration curl work to shape and strengthen the biceps and brachialis muscles.

In order to prevent muscle soreness it's a good idea to

perform one general biceps stretch before you begin your biceps routine.

Biceps Routine

Behind-Back Arm Lift Stretch

This stretch elongates and relaxes the biceps and brachialis muscles. It also relaxes the triceps muscle and the forearm.

◆ **POSITION**

Stand with your feet a natural width apart. Keep your back straight and your head up. Look straight ahead. Lace your fingers together behind your back, with your palms facing the floor.

◆ **STRETCH**

Pull your shoulders up, and, at the same time, use your interlocked hands to pull your arms down until you feel a full stretch in your biceps muscle. Hold the position for three seconds.

◆ **TIMING**

Do the stretch three times.

◆ **TIPS**

Beware of the tendency to tense your neck muscles while performing this stretch. Relax your neck and shoulders.

Do not look down. Keep your eyes straight ahead throughout the stretch.

Resist the temptation to bend and flex your elbows during the stretch. Don't cheat.

It is easy to forget which muscle you're stretching with this movement. Keep your mind riveted on your biceps muscles as you work.

Biceps Exercise #1
Concentration Curl

~~~~~~

The concentration curl strengthens, shapes, and defines the entire biceps and brachialis area, especially the peak of the biceps muscle.

✦ **POSITION**

Bend at the waist with your feet about twelve inches apart. Hold a dumbbell, palm away from your body, in your right hand and place your right elbow on the inside of your right knee. Extend your arm straight down.

✦ **MOVEMENT**

Keeping your body in the bent position, curl the dumbbell upward until it reaches about chin height. (Do not raise your head.) Flex (squeeze) your biceps muscle and return to start position. Feel the stretch in your biceps muscle and repeat the movement until you have completed your set. Repeat the set for the other arm.

✦ **TIPS**

Beware of the temptation to sit up during the exercise. Maintain your bent-at-the-waist stance. Concentrate as you flex and stretch your working muscle. Watch the muscle bulge and elongate.

Concentration curl, start

Concentration curl, finish

Biceps Exercise #2
Standing Alternate Hammer Curl

The hammer curl strengthens, shapes, and defines the biceps and brachialis muscles. It also strengthens the forearm.

✦ POSITION

With a dumbbell in each hand, stand with your feet a natural width apart. Extend your arms straight down at your sides, palms facing your body, and hold each dumbbell touching the sides of your thighs. The dumbbells will be in a "hammerlike" position.

✦ MOVEMENT

Keeping the dumbbells in the hammer position, bend your left arm at the elbow and curl it up toward your left shoulder. When the dumbbell reaches your shoulder, begin to curl the right dumbbell up to your right shoulder while lowering the left dumbbell to start position. Continue this alternating hammerlike movement until you've completed your set.

✦ TIPS

Keep the dumbbell in the hammer position throughout the exercise.

Remember to flex your biceps muscles on the up movement and to stretch them on the down movement.

Do not allow your body to rock from side to side. Keep steady.

✦ VARIATIONS

You may do the hammer curl both arms at a time, seated or standing.

You may do this exercise standing and leaning over.

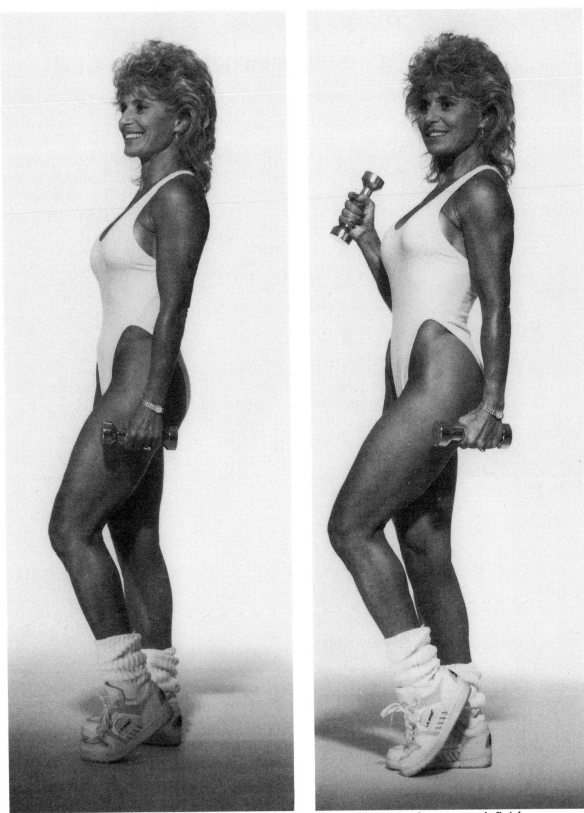

Standing alternate hammer curl, start   Standing alternate hammer curl, finish

Biceps Exercise #3
Standing Alternate Biceps Curl

~~~~~~~~~~~~~~~~~~~~~~~~~~~~~~~~~~~~~~

Perform this exercise exactly as instructed above, only instead of holding the dumbbells in the hammer position (palms facing your body), hold them palms facing forward.

Summary of Biceps Exercises

PRE-WORKOUT STRETCH
Behind-back arm lift

BICEPS ROUTINE
Concentration curl
Standing alternate hammer curl
Standing alternate biceps curl

4 Optional Extras

Optional extras are fun because you don't *have* to do them. You do them because you have the time, energy, and motivation, and you feel great about yourself afterward because you know you went the extra mile.

If you're the type of woman who isn't satisfied with doing only the required amount of anything, or if you're anxious to see results and you want to accelerate your progress, this chapter is for you. On the other hand, if you're quite content with putting in the bare minimum, feel free to skip this chapter—but before you do, please read the following section on aerobics. You owe it to your heart and lungs. It would be to your advantage to make sure that, just when you're finally getting into your best shape, they work with you rather than against you.

Aerobics Every Other Day—The Perfect Companion to Your Workout

You'll be working with weights for thirty minutes every other day in order to shape, firm, and tone the nine major parts of your outer body—but what about your heart and lungs? They need stimulation too—and the best way to keep them in shape is by performing aerobic activities, either no-impact, low-impact, or high-impact. Aerobic activities increase oxygen consumption and endurance, decrease fatigue, increase energy, improve sports and weight-training performance, and burn calories.

Perhaps the best thing about aerobic activities is that they're fun. What's more, there's a great variety. You can run, swim, jump rope, bound on a trampoline, row, ski, water-ski, race walk, walk at a fast pace, dance, aerobic dance, ride a bicycle, ride a stationary bicycle, run stairs, use the StairMaster, use the NordicTrack machine, roller skate, ice skate, and, if you move quickly enough and do it for a long enough time, even your favorite sport.

As long as you keep your heart rate up between sixty and eighty-five percent of capacity for at least twenty minutes, you've accomplished an aerobic effect. (Your maximum pulse rate is calculated by subtracting your age from 220.)

High-impact, No-impact, and Low-impact Aerobics

What? No-impact aerobics? That's right. Swimming, biking, and rowing are no-impact aerobic activities because they do not strain, pound, or shock the muscles, bones, or joints. Swimming takes place in the water, so ballistic movements are eliminated; and biking and rowing are done on an apparatus, so the feet are not touching the ground. Yet they are as effective as any other type of aerobic activity in burning fat and keeping the heart and lungs in shape—depending, of course, upon the intensity with which the workout is performed.

High-impact aerobics includes running, jumping (rope or on the trampoline), stair-climbing, skiing, high-impact aerobic dancing, etc. Any activity that causes you to bounce, jolt, or jump (remove two feet from the ground at one time) is considered to be high-impact aerobics and can, over time, if not used with caution, cause damage to your joints.

Low-impact aerobics include aerobic dance (also called low-percussive dance, protective aerobics, no-bounce dancing, and soft and fluid aerobics), walking, and cross-country skiing.

Low-impact aerobic dance is a lot safer than full-impact aerobic dance because it is not ballistic; at no point do both feet leave the ground. This reduces the impact shock on muscles and joints. Instead, one moves the upper and/or lower body in a wide range of motion.

It has been demonstrated that low-impact aerobic-dance classes can be very effective in improving overall fitness. A recent study shows that women over fifty experienced a twenty-three percent improvement in overall fitness after having participated in a low-impact aerobic-dance program for six years. They did not experience the "normal" functional declines common to women in their fifties. Low-impact aerobics has also proved to help prevent osteoporosis (the progressive thinning and weakening of the bones).

Low-impact aerobic-dance classes are ideal for those who enjoy socializing while working out. For some, engaging in physical activity with others makes the time fly—and the activity turns into fun rather than work. On the other hand, some people treasure time alone and prefer to perform their physical activity in solitude.

Walking is the ideal low-impact aerobic activity for those who enjoy the quietness and privacy of a walk just as the dawn is breaking. It affords them a priceless opportunity to commune with nature.

The great joy of walking is, you can literally stop to smell the roses or inhale the intoxicating aroma of the mimosa trees. Even if you don't actually stop, you won't be speeding past them in a frenzied run, so at least you can inhale their lovely essence. Such moments can reach deep into the soul and remind one what life is all about—the joy of living from moment to moment, and the appreciation of the wonderful universe in all of its natural beauty.

What's more, nothing is more revitalizing than a brisk walk. Every muscle fiber comes alive as you move along. The mind-body connection quickly kicks in. You begin to think creatively. Suddenly the answer to a problem you've been grappling with comes to mind—seemingly out of nowhere. There's something quite magical about a long walk. It clears the mind and makes way for new thoughts.

Which Activity Is Best?

Physiologically, you can gain an equal benefit from any of the aerobic activities—whether no-impact, low-impact or high-impact. It will all depend upon the intensity and length of time you work. Naturally, the greater the intensity and the more time you work, the more calories you'll burn and the greater the benefit will be to your heart and lungs. However, there is good news. It used to be generally agreed upon that one had to keep one's heart rate up to at least seventy to eighty-five percent of maximum capacity for twenty minutes or longer in order to gain an aerobic effect. But it has now been discovered that even sixty percent of the maximum is sufficient for a significant aerobic effect. The American College of Sports Medicine suggests one can improve cardiorespiratory endurance if one gets the heart rate up to about sixty percent of maximum capacity and keeps it there for twenty or more minutes. This means that if you choose a low-intensity activity such as walking, you can still gain an aerobic effect.

The best choice is the safest one that suits your personality, physical well-being, and ability. Low-impact aerobics are of course the safest if you're thinking not only of the short run, but the long run. Low-impact aerobics is the better choice for older women, especially if they've experienced bone loss or have trouble with the spine or their joints. In some cases, even low-impact aerobics can jar the spine or cause excessive flexion to the back. In such cases, an extremely low-impact aerobic activity such as walking, or even a no-impact activity such as swimming, would be best.

Even if you're a younger woman, have experienced no bone loss, and aren't having trouble with your back or your joints, you may want to think twice about engaging in excessive high-impact activities. After all, you may be able to run five miles a day now, but who knows how much damage you are doing to your joints? Please don't misunderstand. We're not trying to suggest that all high-impact aerobic activities are detrimental. We're just saying that medically it's much safer to opt for the no- or low-impact activities.

After all is said and done, take everything into consideration and choose the activity that suits your needs. Obviously, if you have troublesome knees you should not choose running, even if you love to run. And if you're suffering from osteoporosis, you'll avoid high-impact aerobics, because you'll find the impact harmful and painful to your joints. Somewhere within the realm of choices there is a best choice for you.

The Fat-burning Power of Aerobics

In addition to all the wonderful benefits of aerobics mentioned above, aerobic activities are also the most effective of all exercises in burning the body substance that women hate most—fat.

When you're continuously moving through air at a steady pace, your body takes about sixty percent of its fuel from the excess fat in your body and only about forty percent of its fuel from the excess carbohydrates. (This is in contrast to an anaerobic activity such as weight training where your body takes only about forty percent of its fuel from the fat in your body and about sixty percent from the carbohydrates.)

What does all of this mean? While anaerobic activities such as weight training are absolutely necessary to shape and tone the body, and while they do burn a significant amount of body fat, aerobic activities are a must if you wish to get rid of that last bit of unsightly fat.

The Ideal Plan: Alternate-day Aerobic-type Activity

We're not being fair. Here we promised that you'd only have to work out for thirty minutes every other day and you'd be able to tighten, tone, and shape your entire body. Now we're telling you that you really should work out on the alternate days too. What's going on here?

Well, we didn't lie to you. The fact is, even if you didn't do the aerobics or sports activities on the alternate day, you would still reshape your body. However, you would not be able to condition your heart and lungs. After all, you wear them inside your body, and no one but you knows whether or not they're surrounded by fat (you know this when you become out of breath too quickly, etc.). Also, if you don't engage in the alternate-day aerobic activities, it may take longer to get rid of the excess fat that stubbornly clings to your body. As mentioned above, aerobic activities are most effective in the fat-burning area.

So the choice is yours.

Possible Alternate-day Aerobics Plans

Monday	Day 1	Chest, shoulders, triceps, abdominals, and calves
Tuesday	Free Day	30 minutes of brisk walking
Wednesday	Day 2	Thighs, hips/buttocks, back, and biceps
Thursday	Free Day	30 minutes of bicycle riding
Friday	Day 1	Chest, shoulders, triceps, abdominals, and calves
Saturday	Free Day	30-minute low-impact aerobics class
Sunday	Relax	Even God took a day off!
Monday	Day 2	Thighs, hips/buttocks, back, and biceps
Tuesday	Free Day	30 minutes of indoor skiing machine
Wednesday	Day 1	Chest, shoulders, triceps, abdominals, and calves
Thursday	Free Day	30 minutes of swimming
Friday	Day 2	Thighs, hips/buttocks, back, and biceps
Saturday	Free Day	30 minutes of rope jumping
Sunday	Free Day	You know what to do!

You may choose the same or different aerobic activities. For example, you may love walking and decide to walk for thirty or more minutes every other day. Or you may love swimming and choose to do that every alternate day. That's fine. The point is, we prefer that you not totally vegetate on your alternate days!

A Word About Using a Sport as an Aerobic Activity

Yes. You can play tennis, paddleball, squash, or racquetball, volleyball, horseback ride, etc., and count it as your aerobic activity. However, we suggest that you keep moving. Why? Because when you're involved in a sport you're not completely in control of the intensity of the game. You may have to stop or slow down more than you would if you were riding a bicycle, swimming, or jumping rope, for example. But there's no need to be rigid here. If you keep it moving, a swift game of tennis—or any other game, for that matter—will fulfill your aerobic activity.

Tennis, racquetball, volleyball, handball, squash, and other fast-moving ball sports can be aerobic if you keep the intensity up so that you're working at a minimum of fifty percent to sixty percent of your maximal heart rate for at least twenty minutes. But just to be on the safe side, if you're participating in a sport we suggest that you do it for at least forty-five minutes to an hour—what most people do anyway.

Sports that use bursts of energy (start-stop games, such as golf) do not contribute a great deal to cardiovascular fitness, nor do they help burn a significant amount of calories. Yet again, it's better to play golf or some such sport than to sit in a chair and vegetate—a lot better.

Aerobic Activities and Aerobic Sports: Gradual Improvement and Breaking In Gently

There are three phases of progress that take place in the area of aerobic fitness: the initial phase, the improvement phase, and the maintenance phase.

During the initial phase (the first three to eight weeks) you're breaking in to the aerobic activity. Your body is becoming accustomed to the movements and the musculoskeletal coordination required, as well as the aerobic demand.

The next phase, the improvement phase, is where you begin to see changes in your body. Your endurance increases, you experience less shortness of breath, and you don't become exhausted as quickly. In addition, you will acquire increased skill in the aerobic activity or sport, so you'll become more relaxed in doing it. You'll continue to improve for about four to six months.

At about seven months you'll reach your maintenance phase. Now you'll make slight improvements over time—or you'll maintain what you've achieved. In any case, you won't lose ground if you keep up your alternate-day aerobic activity.

It's a good idea to break in as gently as possible if you're going to participate in an aerobic activity or an aerobic sport. Start out by warming up for about five minutes. During this time you can stretch your Achilles tendon, your quadriceps (front thigh muscles), hamstrings (back thigh muscles), and your lower back (see stretches in Chapter 3), and you can walk. Then you may perform your regular or low-intensity aerobic activity for about ten to twelve minutes. If you cannot sustain the activity for that long because you are extremely out of shape, simply begin at a level you can work at. It may be five minutes, it may be even less. Don't worry. In time you'll make considerable progress.

Allow yourself a three-minute cool-down period where you walk again and stretch your quadriceps, hamstrings, and your Achilles tendon.

After you feel comfortable with this level of challenge, add on two minutes after each third workout, until you've reached your goal of twenty or more minutes (up to forty-five minutes maximum).

Everyone Is Different

You may not be able to sustain even a ten-minute aerobic session in the beginning. Don't worry. People of every age differ in their levels of physical fitness. If you have been athletic and physically active all of your life, you are going to achieve your aerobic-fitness goal much more quickly than your couch-potato counterpart, and vice versa.

No matter how out of shape you are, you'll eventually improve your aerobic fitness by twenty percent and more. Start out with less than ten minutes of aerobics if your body is telling you that ten minutes is too much. Three or four minutes will do just fine, as long as you continually increase the amount as your body tells you it's getting stronger.

Will It Be Easy?

No. It won't be easy, because it's human nature to opt for the path of least resistance. Your body and your mind are going to fight you every step of the way when you try to push yourself beyond your already established boundaries of physical effort. However, the only way to make progress is to take control of your body and force it to go a bit further when you feel it's time.

It doesn't matter how old a woman is when she starts an aerobic-exercise program, because all women who exercise can gain fitness benefits. What is important, however, is that women who want to participate in aerobic exercise know how to calculate their target heart rate, understand their own limitations, and be motivated to continue exercising. Older women (those over fifty) and those who have led a sedentary life-style should seek medical supervision before starting any exercise program, whether it be resistance training or aerobics.

The goal for any aerobic workout is to raise the heart rate to between sixty and eighty-five percent of maximum capacity. As mentioned earlier in this chapter, the maximum heart rate is calculated by subtracting your age from 220. You may then figure out sixty percent of that figure, eighty percent of that figure, and so on. Your answer will be the number of times your heart should beat per minute when it is up to that level.

Women under the age of forty tend to train at higher intensities than older women. Since maximal oxygen consumption decreases as a woman ages, an older woman's ability to adjust to fitness programs can take longer. By no means does this indicate that women over forty should not exercise. Quite the contrary. It means that women over forty must be patient and work a little longer in order to see results. In addition, it means that older women are liberated from the obligation to compare themselves and to compete with women ten and twenty years younger than they, even though we must admit that many of us (the authors, for example) cannot help but notice that we're in better aerobic shape than most women twenty years our junior, and you (other older women) can be too! But we're not doing it to compete with our younger counterparts. We're working at our capacity to be our best, and that's just where it happens to land us.

There's another factor that must be taken into consideration. As people age they are subject to more ailments. Unfortunately, some of us have to battle with diabetes, arthritis, asthma, and heart problems. True, younger people often have these problems too, but as time goes by we're more prone to these diseases. We must not despair and throw up our hands in defeat, but face the physical hindrance as an obstacle to be overcome. We must forge ahead and do everything in our power to lead the best possible life until the very last breath we take.

Accelerating Your Progress—Advanced Techniques

For those of you who are impatient, we have good news. You can see results faster by putting in a little extra time. Here are some suggestions.

Work Out Four, Five, or Six Days a Week

Instead of doing the alternate-day workout, work out every day, taking only one day of rest. Since this is a split routine (see Chapter 2 for explanation) you can work out as many days in a row as you wish without overworking your muscles. You, of course, may still do your aerobic or sports activities.

Do Four, Five, or Six Exercises per Body Part

Do the suggested variation exercise for one of the exercises of a given body part. For example, your chest routine requires three exercises: the flat dumbbell press, the flat dumbbell flye, and the cross-bench pullover. If you wish, do four exercises for that body part—the three suggested exercises plus one of the variations. For example, for the chest routine, each of the following alternates are suggested: the incline dumbbell or barbell press, the incline dumbbell flye, and the one-arm cross-bench pullover.

You can add the extra exercise after you've broken in gently with the regular routine (after about two weeks of training or any time after that). If you choose to do four exercises for the chest, it will bring your total workout time up to forty-five minutes. You may even want to go further and do five or six exercises, using two or three of the alternatives. In this case your workout time will be an hour or an hour and fifteen minutes.

Do Four Sets per Body Part

We require that you do three sets per body part. In order to intensify your workout you can add a set to each body part. If you do this using one of the regular routines of three exercises per body part, it will increase your workout time by about seven minutes. If you really want to go wild, you can add one exercise per body part and do four sets for each part. This will increase your total workout time to about an hour.

If you choose to do four sets per body part, remember to break in gently to that addition. Add the fourth set only after having worked out for about two months.

The Pyramid System—Pyramid the Weights and Do Five Sets per Body Part

This method of working out is capable of stimulating muscle growth to the maximum. By adding weight to each set until you reach your capacity, then reducing the weight in each set until you've returned to your starting weight, you force your muscle to work up to its absolute maximum—but without undue strain. In a sense, you "coax" the muscle into working harder. In addition, it's difficult to become bored when you use the pyramid system, because you never do the same thing for two sets. You're always changing both weights and repetitions. In effect, there's no monotony involved and no opportunity to become bored. Here's how it works, using your flat dumbbell flye as an example.

> Set 1: 15 repetitions with 5 lbs.
> Set 2: 12 repetitions with 10 lbs.
> Set 3: 10 repetitions with 15 lbs.
> Set 4: 12 repetitions with 10 lbs.
> Set 5: 15 repetitions with 5 lbs.

This system causes your muscle to work to its maximum capacity. Using the above example, just when you've reached your maximum weight on the dumbbell flye of fifteen pounds at ten repetitions and are tempted to quit, you realize that you can once again use a lighter weight and don't mind continuing the work—even though it will mean doing a few extra reps. The same reasoning follows for the final set, where you're asked to return to fifteen repetitions with five pounds. If you drew the picture of your weights and repetitions on a graph, you would see that you've gone up and down—creating a true pyramid.

You can use the pyramid system for your chest, shoulders, triceps, biceps, back, calves, and thighs. You cannot pyramid abdominal or hips/buttocks exercises, since these body parts are worked with little or no weight.

The Modified Pyramid System—Pyramid the Weights and Do Three Sets per Body Part

For those of you who are not as ambitious, yet want to challenge the muscle a little more than the regular workout does, the modified pyramid system is for you. You can use it whether you're performing two, three, or four exercises per body part. Here's how it works, using the chest workout as an example.

Set 1: 15 repetitions with 5 lbs.
Set 2: 10 repetitions with 10 lbs.
Set 3: 6 to 8 repetitions with 15 lbs.

As you can see, the difference between the regular pyramid system and the modified pyramid system is that instead of descending the pyramid, you stop once you reach its peak. You're able to increase your weight with each set, however, because fewer repetitions are required.

Whether you choose either the regular or the modified pyramid system, remember to maintain the strictest form possible and continually tense your muscles as you work. The idea is not to sacrifice form for added work.

Also, if you choose to pyramid your weights, be sure to select a challenging weight so you don't lose the efficacy of the workout. For example, if you choose one-pound dumbbells for your first set (in anticipation of having to raise your weights for your second and third sets) when you really could handle ten-pound weights, you'll only be fooling yourself. The idea is to challenge the muscles to the maximum of their capacity for each set by selecting a heavy enough weight to cause difficulty after the required amount of reps.

Work in Supersets

A superset is the combination of two sets of two specific exercises with no rest in between. Here's how it works, using the chest routine as an example.

Do Set 1 of the flat dumbbell flye and Set 1 of the flat dumbbell press. Rest 30 seconds.
Do Set 2 of the flat dumbbell flye and Set 2 of the flat dumbbell press. Rest 30 seconds.
Do Set 3 of the flat dumbbell flye and Set 3 of the flat dumbbell press. Stop.

You have now completed two of the exercises in your chest routine. Perform your third exercise in the usual fashion. You can perform the superset for any body part.

The advantage of the superset is twofold. First of all, you save time (a minute and a half in this example). Multiply this by five (if you're working five body parts that day) and you've saved seven and a half minutes. Also, supersets intensify your workout. You challenge the muscle to the maximum by giving it less time to rest.

Another way to do supersets is to mix and match body parts. Here are some mix-and-match superset combinations:

Chest and shoulders
Shoulders and triceps
Triceps and biceps
Chest and triceps
and so on.

Doing supersets in this manner is not as challenging as doing them for a specific body part, because when you're working on the other body part the first one is allowed to rest. However, it's a great way to prevent workout boredom and at the same time intensify the workout.

Work in Giant Sets of Three

The giant set is really an enlarged superset. Instead of doing two exercises at a time you'll be doing three. Here's how it works using the chest routine as an example.

Do Set 1 of the flat dumbbell flye, Set 1 of the flat dumbbell press, and Set 1 of the cross-bench pullover. Rest 30–60 seconds.
Do Set 2 of the flat dumbbell flye, Set 2 of the flat dumbbell press, and Set 2 of the cross-bench pullover. Rest 30–60 seconds.
Do Set 3 of the flat dumbbell flye, Set 3 of the flat dumbbell press, and Set 3 of the cross-bench pullover. Stop.

Naturally, the giant set is even more challenging than the superset. You can make it a little easier by mixing giant sets between body parts. For example, you can choose giant-set exercises from chest, shoulders, and triceps, biceps, triceps;

biceps, triceps, and shoulders; or chest, biceps, and triceps; and so on.

Learn to Burn Extra Calories

You can burn additional calories and get some exercise without ever going out of your way! Instead of taking the elevator or escalator, take the stairs. Instead of spending fifteen minutes looking for the closest parking spot, park a ten-minute walk away. If that means you will be carrying a package back to your car for ten minutes, great. Instead of sitting while you're talking on the telephone, stand.

When working around the house, think energy expenditure rather than energy saving. Rather than hire someone to cut your lawn, do it yourself, and do it with a hand-powered mower rather than a self-propelled mower. In this way you will exercise the muscles of your legs, back, shoulders, and arms.

When working inside, don't think of vacuuming as a dreaded chore, view it as an exercise spurt. Dusting, polishing, washing windows, and even cleaning the stove or the refrigerator involve many upper-body muscles. The fact is, every time you move around and do work, you benefit your body. You're not doing yourself any favors when you hire someone to do everything for you so you can lie on a daybed and take your ease. You'll only have to make it up in extra aerobic and resistance exercises. Let the natural course of life take care of some of your exercise for you.

Conquering Troublesome Body Parts

You may use any or all of the above methods on your entire body, except, as mentioned before, the pyramid system for hips/buttocks and abdominals, since no weight is required for those exercises.

However, if you're like most women, you probably feel that certain body parts need more work than others. If this is true you can choose some of the above methods for your especially troublesome body parts.

For example, most women feel their hips/buttocks, thighs, and abdominals need additional work. Here's a suggested program for "bombing" those body parts.

Additional Exercises for Hips/Buttocks, Thighs, and Abdominals

Do all suggested exercises plus the variation for each of these body parts. Further increase the load by adding a fourth and even fifth set to each exercise.

See also *The Fat-Burning Workout* and *Gut Busters* in Bibliography for additional exercises.

Additional Repetitions for Hips/Buttocks and Abdominals

Instead of doing three sets of fifteen to twenty-five repetitions for hips/buttocks and abdominal exercises, do four or five sets of twenty-five to fifty repetitions.

Additional Workout Days for Hips/Buttocks, Abdominals, and Thighs

You can add your hips/buttocks, abdominals, and thighs on to your upper-body workout day. If you do this you'll be exercising these body parts every other day, and you'll double your progress.

Exercise Your Hips/Buttocks and Abdominals Six Days a Week

Unlike any of the other nine body parts, hips/buttocks and abdominals can be exercised every twenty-four hours. Why? The goal is not to build a muscle there but rather to tighten, tone, and get rid of excess fat. For this reason, you could exercise them six days a week, taking only one day off to prevent burnout.

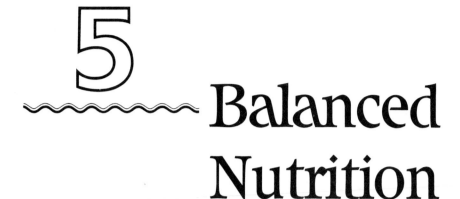

5 Balanced Nutrition

"Lose ten pounds in four days." "Eat your way to thinness with eggs and grapefruit." "The Ice Cream Diet." We've all heard of some miracle weight-loss program, one that promises dramatic results in a matter of days if we're willing to either eat a strange combination of foods or starve ourselves. Trouble is, the plan never works—unless your only goal is to keep the weight off for a week or two.

We have to be honest with you. There is no shortcut to a lean, healthy body. The only way to lose excess weight and keep it off is to continually offer the body a well-balanced, nutritious, low-fat selection of foods. Any other plan is bound to backfire sooner or later.

Total deprivation of one food substance will only make the body crave that substance more. Quick weight loss teaches the body to conserve energy and slows down the metabolism (in other words, teaches the body how to retain as much fat as possible, as insurance against possible future starvation periods). Trick diets that depend on an overbalance of one food substance over another (high-protein, low-carbohydrate diets, for example) produce a temporary weight loss—water—that is quickly regained once the diet is over.

How Fast Will You Lose Weight?

In the following paragraphs we'll show you how to eat so you lose a steady pound to a pound and a half of fat (not water or lean muscle) a week (average) over time. Does that sound like too slow a weight loss? Not when you consider the fact that you won't gain it back. The body loses and gains weight slowly. Come of think of it, you didn't gain an average of more than a pound to a pound and a half a week last year, did you? If you did, you would have gained between fifty-two and seventy-eight pounds last year. If you try to fight the body's natural weight-loss process, you'll be working against nature.

Fortunately, the body is willing to give up excess weight more quickly than it is to put it on. This is understandable, because the body tends to strive toward health. In other words, the body is reluctant to pile on mounds of excess weight, because this is a threat to the heart. In fact, most people gain an average of about one half pound a week— no matter how much they eat (about twenty-six pounds a year). You will lose more than an average of one half pound a week. This is true because when the body is carrying excess weight its goal is to rid itself of that weight as quickly as possible, but not so quickly as to pose a threat to survival. As mentioned earlier, you will lose an average of a pound to a pound and a half a week. To try to lose more quickly will invite failure. You cannot work against nature. The body's natural survival system will force you to binge at some point if you try to rush weight loss.

The reason this food plan works is simple. It allows you to eat nutritious foods in a balanced combination so your body can function to its optimum ability. In a matter of weeks your body will crave this food plan and will cooperate with you one hundred percent. You will no longer be continually tempted to eat high-fat, non-nutritious foods.

In order to understand the makings of a well-balanced diet, it is necessary to comprehend the basic food elements and how they are utilized by the body.

Calories

A dietary calorie is a unit of energy available in a specified food. Technically speaking, a calorie is the amount of heat (or energy) necessary to raise the temperature of one gram of water one degree Celsius. It takes one thousand calories to equal a dietary calorie, or "Kcal." For the purpose of simplicity, when discussing food most writers simply use the word "calorie" instead of using the technical term "Kcal."

Protein and carbohydrates both contain four calories per gram, while fat contains more than double that amount— nine calories per gram. Our bodies need the energy produced by dietary calories in order to function. We need calories not only to walk, run, and do work, but even to breathe.

When we aren't getting enough calories to sustain our basic life functions, our bodies begin to use reserve calories. When we're consuming more calories than we need for daily use, our bodies begin to store them up for future use in the form of fat, which is deposited under our skin. When we store up an extreme amount of calories, we begin to look "fat."

Protein

Without protein we would not be able to grow or heal. Protein is the food element responsible for building our bodies. Protein comprises our muscles and much of our hair, fingernails, skin, ligaments, enzymes (such as saliva), blood, immune cells, and internal organs. Protein plays a role in regulating the acid-alkaline balance of the blood and tissues and in regulating the body's water balance. It is also an essential element in the production of hormones, which control metabolism, growth, and sexual development.

When digested, protein is broken down into smaller units called amino acids. The human body needs twenty-two amino acids to make the protein usable to it. The human body can manufacture all but eight of these units without the aid of an outside source. However, to produce the other eight, which have come to be called "essential amino acids," the body must be supplied with poultry, red meat, pork (we do not recommend the latter two), fish, dairy products, eggs, or special combinations such as soybeans and rice, or corn and milk.

Our bodies require a continual supply of protein, because unlike fat or carbohydrates, protein cannot be stored in the body for future use. For this reason, it's a good idea to eat protein in small amounts two or three times a day rather than in large amounts all at once. A healthy amount of protein is about one-half gram daily per pound of body weight. For example, if you weigh 120 pounds you should consume about 60 grams of protein per day. In terms of calories, since a gram of protein contains four calories, you will be consuming about 240 calories of protein per day. If you're on a weight-loss plan you'll probably be consuming about 1,500 calories a day. This means that you're consuming about sixteen percent of your total diet from protein. This is a good balance. You'll consume the rest of your calories from fat and carbohydrates (about twenty percent from fat and the rest, about sixty-four percent, from carbohydrates).

Protein, when consumed in excess, is eliminated in the urine. To facilitate the elimination of excess protein it's a good idea to drink lots of water (six to eight glasses a day).

Carbohydrates

Carbohydrates include a large category of foods: simple carbohydrates (sugars) and complex carbohydrates (vegetables and fiber). Carbohydrates are the main source of energy to the body and the brain.

The less desirable carbohydrates are simple sugars (sucrose, fructose, lactose, dextrose, and others), because they require little expenditure of digestive energy to be broken down into blood glucose. They contain single or very few sugar molecules, as opposed to complex carbohydrates, which contain multiple natural sugar molecules and require more enzymatic degradation for digestion.

Simple carbohydrates are not the best carbohydrates, because they're converted into glucose (potential energy) so quickly that they produce an immediate boost of energy. However, there's a price to be paid for this quick shot of power. About twenty minutes after consuming a simple carbohydrate the blood sugar drops a bit lower than it was before the carbohydrate was consumed, and a feeling of fatigue along with an urge to consume more simple carbohydrates follows. This can lead to a vicious circle of eating more and more simple carbohydrates, significantly adding to the calorie count—and eventually to stored fat.

Fruit is the best source of simple carbohydrates because it carries with it vitamins, minerals, and fiber. Processed simple carbohydrates such as refined sugar, candy, jams, and jellies are less desirable because they offer little or no nutritional value.

Complex carbohydrates are the best source of energy and nutrition because they offer the body a supply of gradually released energy. In essence, complex carbohydrates are exactly as described—complex. They are a combination of many simple sugars. Due to the nature of the multiple bonding they require more work by the digestive system for breakdown and use. Because it takes longer for complex carbohydrates to be broken down by the digestive system, they do not raise the blood sugar level suddenly.

The advantage of this is twofold. There is no quick energy boost and concomitant letdown and need for another "fix," and you can go for a longer period of time without having to eat again than if you'd consumed simple carbohydrates.

There is yet another advantage in consuming the majority of your calories from complex carbohydrates. It takes more energy to metabolize complex carbohydrates than it does to metabolize other foods. Current research indicates that it requires twenty-five percent more calories for the body to digest and metabolize complex carbohydrates than it does for the same amount of fat. The simple fact is, one hundred calories of a complex carbohydrate are not as "fattening" as one hundred calories of fat. In essence, twenty-five of the calories in the complex carbohydrates disappear before they're available for energy use or fat storage.

As mentioned above, your total carbohydrate intake should be about sixty-four percent of your diet.

Fiber

Fiber is found in carbohydrates. There are two types of fiber: soluble fiber (oat bran, psyllium, fresh fruits, vegetables, and legumes), which can be digested by humans, and insoluble fiber (whole wheat, whole grains, corn meal, brown rice), which cannot be digested by humans (because of the makeup and combination of the glucose molecules). Each type of fiber has its own distinct advantage. Soluble fiber can help to lower blood sugar and cholesterol levels.

It has recently been discovered in studies conducted by the American Cancer Society that people who consume a lot of insoluble fiber significantly reduce their chances of developing stomach, colon, and rectal cancer. Why?

When a significant amount of insoluble fiber is consumed, stool volume is multiplied (as much as three times). This helps prevent constipation and also causes the concentration of bile acids to be diluted. While bile acids are necessary for the digestion of fat, they are also possible catalysts to colon cancer, so this watering-down effect is extremely desirable.

The RDA recommendation for fiber is about thirty grams per day. Here are the fiber counts for some foods.

1 oz. bran flakes-type cereal	9 g
1 slice whole-wheat bread	2 g
1 slice cracked-wheat bread	2 g
1 slice rye bread	1 g

(In contrast, a slice of white bread has only ½ g of fiber.)

FRESH FRUITS

Orange	5 g
Pear	5 g

Banana	4 g
1 cup strawberries	4 g
Apple	3.5 g

FRESH VEGETABLES

For one cup of each of the following vegetables:

Spinach	11 g
Peas	8 g
Corn	8 g
Broccoli	6 g
Carrots	5 g
Eggplant	5 g
Cabbage	4 g
Green beans	4 g
Tomato	4 g
Cauliflower	2 g

Celery, green peppers, and lettuce yield relatively little fiber compared with the above vegetables, about 1 g per cup. However, these vegetables are rich in other important vitamins and minerals (see list later in this chapter).

BEANS AND LEGUMES

These are rich sources of fiber. One cup of baked beans or split peas yields about 21 g of fiber, and lentils yield 18 g of fiber per cup.

Fat

We've saved the most notorious of the three food elements for last. Of late, fat has become an outlaw in the food world, and rightly so. Whereas the other two food elements, protein and carbohydrates, yield only four calories per gram, fat yields nine. Whereas the other two use up twenty percent of their own calories in the digestion process, fat uses up only about three percent. Whereas the other two can speed up the metabolism when consumed, fat can slow it down. Whereas the other two are quickly used as energy, fat is quickly stored as fat. In other words, the cliché is true: Fat goes straight to your hips.

How the Body Uses Fat

In addition to providing the body with its most concentrated source of energy and furnishing the body with insulation against the cold, fat functions to carry certain vitamins through the digestive system: A, D, E, and K. Fats assist in converting carotene to vitamin A, and they make calcium available to bones and teeth by helping the body absorb vitamin D.

When fat is consumed, the stomach's secretion of hydrochloric acid is slowed down and digestion is prolonged. For this reason, consumption of high-fat foods tends to create a feeling of fullness that lasts a long time. You may have noticed that when you eat a high-fat meal such as beef or fried foods, you feel sluggish for some time afterward.

The Difference between Saturated and Unsaturated Fat

Both saturated and unsaturated fats are called fatty acids. Saturated fatty acids become solid at room temperature and are derived, with the exception of coconut oil, from animal sources. Excessive consumption of saturated fats is dangerous to your health. Recent studies indicate that women who consume a lot of this type of fat are three times more likely to develop breast cancer than women who eat a low-fat diet. It's important to get into the habit of reading food labels. New laws require that foods be carefully labeled as to fat content. A notorious food offender in the world of fats is the frankfurter—beef, chicken, or turkey. If you read the label you'll find about seventy percent of the total calories in a hot dog come from saturated fat.

Unsaturated fatty acids become liquid at room temperature. They are derived from nuts, seeds, and vegetables. High consumption of these fats can also be detrimental to your health, but not as detrimental as the unsaturated variety.

Cholesterol

Cholesterol is a type of fat. It helps to form the sex and adrenal hormones, vitamin D, and bile. It is also a component of cell membranes and nerve linings and is found in the brain, liver, and blood. Only about half of the cholesterol found in the blood comes from the diet. The other half comes from synthesis that occurs in the liver and intestines.

What's the Difference between Good Cholesterol and Bad Cholesterol?

As you might have heard by now, not all cholesterol is bad for you. Cholesterol is divided into two categories: HDL and LDL.

Both HDL and LDL are composed of lipoproteins, molecular structures made of fats (lipids) and proteins bonded together with cholesterol. These little packets travel through the bloodstream.

The LDL packet functions to carry cholesterol from its place of synthesis to cell membranes, where it is needed for maintenance of the cells. LDL also carries cholesterol through the arterial walls, and herein lies the problem. If an overabundance of LDL is carried through the arterial walls, it will eventually become deposited on the walls as plaque. When this happens, in time the arterial walls become too narrow to allow blood to freely pass through. End result: heart disease and possible heart failure.

HDL is called "good cholesterol" because it removes cholesterol from the tissues and carries it back to the liver, where it is transformed into bile acids and excreted into the intestine.

Not too long ago people assumed that as long as their overall cholesterol level was under 200, they had nothing to worry about. They also assumed that if their cholesterol level was well over 200 they were in serious trouble. Today we know it is not that simple. The person with the lower count can in fact be in more trouble than the person with the higher count, depending upon the ratio of total cholesterol to HDL.

In order to find out the status of your cholesterol condition, you must ask your doctor for a fractionated cholesterol test. This test measures your total cholesterol against your HDL. The doctor then prepares a ratio. For example, if your total cholesterol count is 200 and your HDL is 50, your risk level is 4 (50 goes into 200 four times). This is a good risk level. On the other hand, if your total cholesterol count is 200 but your HDL is only 25, your risk level is 8 (25 goes into 200 eight times). This is a very high risk level.

The most natural question to ask at this point is, how can one raise the HDL level? To date, the only proven way to raise HDL is to regularly participate in vigorous exercise, such as prescribed in this workout. Scientists are presently working on other ways to raise HDL. Many doctors believe keeping saturated fat low and limiting smoking and drinking can help raise HDL.

How Much Fat Should We Consume on a Daily Basis?

In order to remain at maximum health you should restrict your daily fat intake to no more than twenty percent. If you follow the balanced eating plan discussed in this chapter, you'll be getting about twenty percent of your calories from fat, sixteen percent from protein, and sixty-four percent from carbohydrates.

Vitamins and Minerals

Vitamins are micronutrients. They are organic chemicals found in foods. Vitamin deficiencies can wreak havoc upon your health; therefore it is important to be aware of the vitamin content of various foods.

Minerals are nutrients found in organic and inorganic combinations and are needed in much greater amounts by the body than vitamins. Deficiency of various minerals can result in bone disease and problems with the organs and the nervous system. Minerals are found in tap water throughout the United States. If you are one of the many people who have switched to bottled water or a home purifying system, it is especially important for you to either step up your consumption of mineral-rich foods or take a daily mineral supplement.

While it is always best to consume your daily intake of vitamins and minerals from food, it is not always possible. Therefore, most doctors agree that a daily multivitamin and mineral supplement is a good idea.

Sources of Vitamins

VITAMIN A

Broccoli
Carrots
Cheese
Spinach
Eggs
Fish
Liver
Yellow fruits and vegetables

VITAMIN B COMPLEX

Brewer's yeast
Whole grains
Wheat germ
Yogurt
Organ Meats

VITAMIN B1

Wheat germ
Brown rice
Fish
Lobster
Poultry
Organ meats
Nuts

VITAMIN B2

Green leafy vegetables
Fruit
Whole grains
Eggs
Poultry
Legumes
Organ meats

VITAMIN B6

Green leafy vegetables
Bananas
Cabbage
Wheat germ
Whole grains
Organ meats
Beef
Nuts

VITAMIN B12

Milk and milk products
Eggs
Fish
Organ meats
Beef

NIACIN

Whole grains
Breads and cereals
Milk and milk products
Eggs
Seafood
Poultry
Organ meats
Beef

VITAMIN C

All fruits and vegetables, especially oranges (as noted above, oranges are also an excellent source of fiber).

VITAMIN D

Sunlight
Egg yolks
Milk

VITAMIN E

Dark-green vegetables
Fruits
Wheat germ
Organ meats

Calcium

Calcium stands alone as a mineral of great importance, because a lack of it can cause major bone problems later in life. After the age of thirty, women (and men) begin to experience gradual thinning and shortening of the bones. If this happens in the extreme, osteoporosis will occur. There is a way to head off such an eventuality, however, and the remedy is given in this book: exercise and diet.

"Why do I have to exercise if I get enough calcium in my diet?" you may ask. Well, exercise in and of itself not only helps to strengthen and build bone, it also assists your body in absorbing calcium into your bloodstream. Without absorption, even the calcium you do consume would not be useful to you.

The RDA (Recommended Daily Allowance) of calcium as stipulated by the United States Government is 800 to 1,200 milligrams. This suggested amount, however, is the bare minimum. Most doctors recommend a safety amount of 1,500 mg.

Foods on the following list contain 100 mg of calcium per measured amount. Try to include as many of them in your daily diet as possible, especially vegetables, because they also provide much of your daily fiber and vitamin requirements.

1 c. skim milk
8 oz. plain low-fat yogurt
1 c. low-fat cottage cheese
1 oz. part-skim mozzarella cheese
1 oz. low-fat Swiss cheese
1 c. farina
⅔ c. Cream of Wheat cereal
⅔ c. oatmeal
1 c. navy beans
1 c. soybeans
1 c. bean curd (tofu)
10 okra pods
1 c. broccoli
1 c. collard greens
1 c. mustard greens
1 c. dandelion greens
1 c. turnip greens
1 c. kale
4 oz. scallops
4 oz. shrimp

You may never have eaten some of these greens. Well, it's about time you added some variety to your diet. Go to the vegetable stand and stock up. You'll give your taste buds as well as your body a real treat.

Note: While low-fat mozzarella and low-fat Swiss cheese are high in calcium, even the low-fat cheeses are high-fat foods and should not be eaten more than twice a week while you're trying to lose weight. In addition, note that scallops and shrimp are high in cholesterol.

There are other minerals that are vital to your good health. Here is a list of food sources, for your convenience.

Sources of Minerals

IRON
Dark-green leafy vegetables
Wheat germ
Whole grains
Eggs
Fish
Oysters
Shellfish
Poultry
Organ meats

MAGNESIUM
Green vegetables
Brown rice
Bran
Seafood
Organ meats

PHOSPHORUS
Seaweed
Grains
Yogurt
Yellow cheeses
Eggs
Poultry
Fish
Beef

POTASSIUM
Broccoli
Brussels sprouts
Lima beans
Carrots
Spinach
Yellow vegetables
Potatoes
Lettuce
Apples
Bananas
Cantaloupe
Poultry, dark meat
Tuna
Haddock
Eggs
Brown rice

Note: While organ meats are high in needed vitamins and minerals, they are also high in cholesterol. Be aware.

Sodium

Sodium is a needed mineral. However, it has gotten a bad reputation because of its capacity to aggravate hypertension. In addition, because sodium holds up to fifty times its own weight in water, excessive sodium in the diet causes water retention and bloating. The fact is, if you consume too much sodium (more than the RDA of between 1,300 and 3,300 mg.) you will appear five to ten pounds heavier than you really are, because water bloat gives the appearance of fat.

There *is* a difference between water bloat and fat, however. You can get rid of water bloat in a matter of days (five to ten pounds—depending upon how much water you're retaining) by merely cutting back on your sodium intake, whereas it takes weeks and even months of strict dieting and exercise to get rid of unwanted fat.

Sodium is rarely lacking in the diet of most people in the modern world. If anything, it is too much in abundance. Frozen dinners, fast foods, smoked foods, Chinese foods, pickles, and canned foods are primary sources of excessive sodium. Avoid them completely or monitor them closely. If you're purchasing a frozen dinner, be sure to read the label. Most frozen dinners contain at least seven hundred milligrams of sodium per serving.

Nearly all foods contain some sodium—even the nutritious apple, peach, or potato. But they don't have very much. Check the following list for a general idea of sodium content, and consult the labels of foods or *The Corinne T. Netzer Encyclopedia of Food Values* for detailed information on the sodium content of specific foods.

The following table describes the milligrams of sodium for a three-and-a-half-ounce serving of each food:

Apple	2		Chicken	50	
Banana	2		Flounder	80	
Cantaloupe	12		Sole	80	
Orange	1		Salmon	50	
Broccoli	25		Tuna (canned)	300	
Cabbage	20		Bacon	275	
Carrot	35	(canned, 320)	Beef	70	
Celery	25		Bologna	1,300	
Lettuce	4		Corned beef	935	
Peas	1	(canned, 250)	Hamburger	1,050	
Potatoes	3		Eggs	60	
Eggplant	2		Yogurt	130	
Onion	10	(pickled, 1,400)	Milk	60	
Radish	3		American cheese	1,300	
Mushrooms	28	(canned, 425)	Potato chips	995	
Tomatoes	3	(canned, 450)	Worcestershire sauce	820	

As you can see, many food items are too high in sodium for frequent consumption. In addition, it's clear that there's no need to ever sprinkle salt on your food. Just one commercial packet of table salt contains five hundred milligrams of sodium. I'm sure you've seen people add two or three of these, unnecessarily, to their meals.

Spices

Instead of salt, get into the habit of sprinkling spices, lemon juice, and flavored vinegars on your food. Here are some descriptions of various spices and suggestions as to which spices go well with which foods.

BASIL: sweet and aromatic (vegetables)

BAY LEAF: strong and pungent (stews and pot roasts)

CHIVES: onionlike flavor (fish and salads)

CLOVES: pungent (cabbage and lamb)

DILL: picklelike or lemony taste (fish, salads, cabbage)

GARLIC POWDER: tangy and pungent (beef, sauces, etc.)

MARJORAM: minty, sweet, and clovelike (lamb, chicken, eggs)

OREGANO: sweet and clovelike (sauces, chicken, eggplant)

ROSEMARY: pungent, spicy, and bittersweet (beef, lamb, veal)

SAGE: pungent and bitter (soups, stews, stuffings)

TARRAGON: sweet, aromatic, and aniselike (veal, salmon)

THYME: penetrating and powerful (meatloaf, squash, onions)

There are many interesting spices on the supermarket shelves. Why not buy ones you've never even heard of before and experiment? Be creative when it comes to spices. Be adventurous and sprinkle any combination of them into a tossed salad, for example.

Water

Water is the primary carrier of nutrients throughout the body. It is involved in nearly every bodily function, including absorption, digestion, excretion, and circulation. Perhaps that is why two thirds of our body weight is comprised of water. We could go forty days without food, but we could not survive a week without water.

Since we lose about three quarts of water a day through perspiration and excretion, it's crucial that we replace this loss daily. You should drink six to eight glasses of water every day. You'll make up the rest in foods, which are comprised of more than ninety percent water. The best sources of water from foods are fruits and vegetables. The water contained in them is one hundred percent hydrogen and oxygen—nothing else added.

These days many people are reluctant to drink tap water because of possible chemical pollution. If you feel this way you may want to purchase a home water-purification unit or you can buy bottled water. In any case, be sure to drink your minimum daily intake of water.

Another important reason to drink water is to curb the

appetite. A glass of water before each meal takes the edge off hunger and can stop you from eating an extra few hundred calories. In addition, drinking lots of water helps with water retention: The more you drink, the less you will retain, because water helps to flush out the excess sodium in your system. Finally, and most important to some of us, a plentiful daily supply of water helps your skin look young and healthy.

Caffeine and Alcohol

While consumption of caffeine and alcohol in excess is detrimental to your health, unless you have a special problem these substances in moderation will pose no threat to you. Check with your doctor for your particular situation. The general rule is, no more than two or three cups of coffee a day, and no more than one or two servings of an alcoholic beverage per day. *We* do not consume the maximum allowance, however, and we don't advise you to, either. One or two cups of coffee is more than enough, and a drink or two on weekend days is plenty.

Choose a Variety of Foods

Before you even start your eating plan, make up your mind to get out of your food rut. Stop eating the same things week after week and force yourself to try different foods. Try an experiment: Don't repeat a protein main dish, a fruit, or a vegetable for two solid weeks.

At first it'll seem strange and you may fight it, telling yourself it's silly. But it isn't. Why? Because it's boredom that causes most people to break their diets. If you choose from nutritious foods well within the limit of your diet, you won't be as tempted to seek out junk foods. Try another experiment: Eat one food from each group every day for the next two weeks. If you can't stand eating fish every day (we wouldn't blame you), substitute white-meat chicken or turkey for fish every so often. Other than that, keep the variety going. See whether or not you become bored with eating right. We seriously doubt it. In fact, you'll probably wonder why you were in such a food rut in the first place.

Below is a list of suggested foods for daily consumption:

FISH	FRUIT	VEGETABLES
Abalone	Apples	Asparagus
Cod	Apricots	Bamboo shoots
Flounder	Bananas	Beans, green
Haddock	Blackberries	Beans, yellow (wax)
Halibut	Blueberries	Beets

FISH	FRUIT	VEGETABLES
Lobster	Boysenberries	Broccoli
Pike	Cantaloupe	Brussels sprouts
Scallops	Cherries	Cabbage
Shrimp	Grapefruit	Carrots
Snails	Grapes	Celery
Snapper	Honeydew	Chard
Sole	Loganberries	Collards
Swordfish	Nectarines	Endive
Tuna	Peaches	Tomatoes

Most people resent what they call "dieting" because it's limiting. But there's no reason to feel limited. You could eat a different fruit, vegetable, or protein every day for a month without ever repeating one. Get yourself a copy of *The Corinne T. Netzer Encyclopedia of Food Values* and check for food value—then go shopping. Why remain locked in a self-imposed prison? Enjoy the variety that nature has provided for you.

The Weight-Loss Plan

If you follow this plan you should lose an average of one to one and a half pounds per week. In all you will be consuming between 1,250 and 1,500 calories daily, although you will never have to count them.

Note the word "average." No one loses weight at exactly the same pace each week. Most people lose more in the beginning and then slow down a little. The reason for this is twofold:

1) The body releases excess water in addition to fat in the beginning stages of most diets.
2) As your body reaches its weight goal it is less anxious to get rid of stored fat. The survival system encourages it to keep some for possible future famine. Nevertheless, if you are persistent your body will give in. For example, you may lose nothing or even gain a pound for one or two weeks. Then suddenly you will lose two pounds. Be patient.

Since we're not asking you to count calories, how will you know if you're consuming too many or too few? If you wish you may count your calories on a given day, just to see that you're keeping within the 1,500-calorie guideline. Chances are, you'll go under or over it by about 200 calories on certain days. Don't worry about this. The food plan is set up so

no matter what, you will lose weight. This is possible because your fat, sugar, protein, and starchy carbohydrate intake is limited.

Carbohydrates

You may eat as much of the following complex carbohydrates as you please, any time, night or day, with the exception of those marked with an asterisk. You must limit these
to two servings per day.

UNLIMITED VEGETABLES

Asparagus
Bamboo shoots
Beans: green, yellow
Beets
Brussels sprouts
Cauliflower
Celery
Chard
Chives
Collard
*Corn
Cucumber
Eggplant
Endive

Kale
Mushrooms
Mustard greens
Okra
Onions
*Potatoes
Rutabaga
Scallions
Shallots
Spinach
Tomatoes
Turnips, turnip greens
Watercress
*Yams

FRUITS

You may have as many as three but not less than one of
any of the following fruits on a given day. One serving of
the berries, cherries, and pineapple is ½ c. One serving of
the cantaloupe and grapefruit is ½ c. One serving of all
other fruits is one large fruit.

Bananas
Blackberries
Blueberries
Boysenberries
Cantaloupe
Cherries
Grapefruit
Grapes
Nectarine

Orange
Peach
Pear
Persimmon
Pineapple
Raspberries
Strawberries
Tangerine

LIMITED COMPLEX CARBOHYDRATES: BRANS, FLOURS, CEREALS, GRAINS, AND GRAIN PRODUCTS

You may have up to two servings a day.

Bran: 1 muffin or 8 oz. cereal
Buckwheat: 8 oz. cereal
Corn: 1 muffin or 1 slice bread
Pasta: 1 cup cooked—high-protein or whole-wheat
Rice: 1 cup cooked—brown or white
Whole wheat: 2 slices bread or 8 oz. cereal

Protein

LOW-FAT PROTEIN

Choose two to three six-to-eight-ounce servings per day.

Chicken (white meat)
Turkey (white meat)
Crab
Flounder
Haddock
Halibut
Oysters
Perch
Yellow perch
Pike
Pollock
Scallops
Snapper
Tuna
Egg whites (unlimited use)

LIMITED DAIRY PRODUCTS

Cheeses are naturally high in fat (and sodium, too, for that matter). Even though you choose the low-fat varieties the fat content is still high, so except for low-fat cottage cheese, have cheese no more than two times a week (one serving = 1 oz.). You may have one 8-oz. low-fat yogurt once a day, and four eggs per week. You may have up to two 8-oz. glasses of skim milk per day.

Fat

You'll get most of your daily fat requirement in your protein. There's no need to go out of your way and put butter, margarine, cream cheese, or oil (all pure fat) on your foods. For example, there are two and one-half grams of fat in eight ounces of even low-fat fish such as sole or flounder, and about twice as much in the same portion of skinless white-meat chicken. Nevertheless, these are "fat bargains" when you compare them with beef, even "lean" ground beef, which contains twenty-five grams of fat for the same portion. Double that amount for regular ground beef.

Even the innocent apple has one gram, or nine calories, of fat, believe it or not.

Sample Daily Diet Meal Plan

Use this as your model. Change your foods every day in order to keep from becoming bored. Select your diet foods from the foods listed above—adding foods you discover for yourself as you read *The Corinne T. Netzer Encyclopedia of Food Values* (which tells you which foods have the best food value—low fat, lots of vitamins and minerals, etc.).

Breakfast
1 oz. cereal in 1 c. skim milk
1 diced fruit
Coffee with skim milk

Snack
1 c. plain yogurt

Lunch
6 oz. can tuna (in water), made into salad with various chopped vegetables
2 slices whole-wheat toast
Tossed salad
Herbal tea

Snack
1 fruit
Unlimited complex carbohydrates
Seltzer

Dinner
8 oz. skinless broiled chicken breast
Baked potato with yogurt (to replace sour cream)
1 c. selected vegetables
No-calorie beverage

Snack
1 fruit
Unlimited complex carbohydrates

Rules for Creating Your Daily Meal Plans

1. Consume protein at least twice daily.
2. Consume no less than ½ gram of protein per pound of body weight. (If you weigh 120 pounds you will consume 60–80 grams of protein, or 240–320 calories of protein.)
3. Keep your fat intake as low as possible. Never exceed twenty grams of fat per day. Never consume full-fat *anything*.

4. Consume no more than three fruits per day.
5. Consume unlimited complex carbohydrates whenever you are hungry.
6. Consume limited complex carbohydrates no more than twice daily.
7. Eat five or more times a day.
8. Eat no less than every four hours.
9. Drink a glass of water before each meal.
10. Continually change the foods you eat. Select from the above lists.
11. Consume no more than two low-fat cheeses per week.
12. Consume no more than four eggs per week.
13. Consume no more than one yogurt per day and no more than two glasses of skim milk.

When You Reach Your Weight Goal

Once you reach your weight goal, continue to eat as suggested above, but if you wish, you may add high-fat fishes and beef once a week. In addition, you may have cheese four times a week.

You may now choose one day a week for "free eating." On this day you may eat anything you please, all day long. The next day you will return to the eating guidelines mentioned above.

"But won't I gain weight if I eat anything I choose all day long, once a week?" you ask. No. As long as you maintain good eating habits all week, your weekly indulgence will not cause you to gain weight.

What Happens If You Start to Regain Weight?

First of all, don't just go by what the scale says. As mentioned before, scale weight can be tricky. Water weight can fluctuate as much as seven pounds. Also, muscle weighs more than fat, so you may be gaining muscle and losing fat. Base your decision as to whether or not you're gaining fat weight by how your clothing fits and how you look in the mirror in the nude (on a day when you haven't overdone your sodium intake and when you're not expecting your period). If you see that you've really started to regain a few pounds of fat, then go right back to the weight-loss program until you lose it again.

Vacations, Holidays, and Other Extended Eating Occasions

If you want to go to town and eat indiscriminately for a few days, you'll have to give up your free eating day each week for the number of days you splurged. For example, should you eat for four days in a row, stuffing yourself with everything in sight, you will not have a free eating day for four weeks.

But why should you binge for four days? It's totally unnecessary. Even on vacations you could select appropriate foods from the menu and keep your good eating habits—splurging only one or two days of the week. You'll feel better, and you'll look better too. What's more, once you get used to smart eating you'll never again feel you're in danger of gaining weight when on vacation. This will help you to enjoy your vacations that much more.

Balanced Beauty

Overall beauty involves a lot more than having a great body. If you truly want to look beautiful, you should appear rested and relaxed and you should have healthy-looking skin.

The Importance of Sleep

We've all heard the expression "I've got to get my beauty sleep." Well, the saying has its roots in a basic truth: A well-rested face is a beautiful face. A face that has been deprived of needed sleep is a haggard face. So if you want to look your best and take at least three years off your looks, be sure to get between seven and eight hours of sleep a night. The exact amount of sleep you need depends upon your particular needs. Sleep needs vary by as much as two hours.

If you can't get as much sleep as you need, take catnaps. It has recently been discovered that a catnap can revitalize you—even if it's only a fifteen-minute snooze.

The Skin

The skin is the first to give away a woman's age. When a woman reaches her mid-thirties, lines around the corners of the eyes, the upper lip, the forehead, and the cheeks begin to deepen. Why does this happen?

As the skin ages it loses moisture and elasticity. The lubricating fat in the skin redistributes itself, and the facial muscles begin to deteriorate.

Another cause of wrinkling is high cholesterol and high blood pressure. Both high cholesterol and high blood pressure interfere with the skin's natural blood supply. This causes the skin to lose moisture and age prematurely.

Another enemy of the skin is stress. Stress can, believe it or not, cause acne, even in your thirties, forties, or fifties. When you experience stress, the chemical androgen is produced. This chemical causes the oil glands to become overactive, and acne is the result.

Although there's nothing we can do to actually turn back the clock, and although no amount of cosmetic surgery will actually make us twenty years younger, there are facial cosmetic-surgery procedures to make us look great for our age. In our opinion, if you want to opt for cosmetic surgery, as long as you're doing it for the right reasons, there's nothing wrong with it.

Finally, as some of you will find out, even after you get in shape there will still be some faults on your body. Perhaps there will be areas where, no matter how thin you are, a roll of fat stubbornly remains, and the only way you would be able to get rid of it by dieting would be to practically starve yourself. You may also find that there are places on your body where, because of childbirth, extreme weight loss, or just the force of gravity with advancing age, your skin sags in an unsightly manner. If any of these situations apply to you, you may want to opt for cosmetic surgery. As you know by now, of course, cosmetic surgery is never a replacement for exercise and the building of healthy, strong muscles. It is an addition, in special cases.

Keeping the Skin Young

After thirty-five the oil-producing sebaceous glands, which naturally lubricate our skin, start to become less active. For this reason, even if you never used moisturizers when you were younger it's important to begin using them as time goes by.

Soap can dry the skin, especially if, like most Americans, you shower daily. We suggest that you use a simple soap such as Neutrogena, Alpha Keri, Basis, Ivory, or unscented Dove.

Once a week, while you're in the shower, use an abrasive cream or grain on a washcloth or brush and get rid of your "old" skin. The body sheds one layer of skin every day, as the new cells push the older cells to the surface. Rather than leave this top layer of dead cells, which can give your skin the look of age, it's a good idea to remove them. By exfoliating your dead skin cells you can help keep your skin looking young and healthy. Exfoliating your skin will also help it absorb moisturizer more efficiently. (Speak to your dermatologist or regular cosmetics adviser about which exfoliation substance is right for you.)

After you shower, your skin cells are enlarged with water. It's a perfect time to apply a body lotion containing lanolin. This will seal the moisture in. Be sure to apply the lotion to your entire skin surface.

Spices and Alcohol

Unfortunately, some of the things we love to eat and drink contribute to dry skin problems. Too much spice in our foods or an overabundance of coffee or alcohol in our diet can cause the blood vessels in the skin's outer layer to swell, making the skin appear dry and flaky.

Winter Winds

The cold winter wind can dry and chap your skin in a matter of minutes. If you are a skier it's a good idea to coat your face with Vaseline (after applying a sunscreen of at least SPF 15). This way your face will be well protected against the elements.

Sun Damage

Women who have spent a lot of time in the sun in their teens and twenties will find that the lines on their faces begin to show up in their thirties and forties. Why does this happen?

Over a period of time the sun can break down the collagen fibers and, along with it, the fibers that bind the skin together and give it its elastic, recoiling properties. The skin loses elasticity.

In addition, overexposure to the sun can cause skin lesions (brown spots that look like enlarged freckles) and skin cancer. While the skin lesions are usually harmless to your health, they're unappealing to the eye. Unfortunately, some of these skin lesions will not be harmless brown spots, but may in fact be cancerous. If you're concerned, it's a good idea to check with your dermatologist.

The sun is causing more skin cancer today than it did fifty years ago. Why is this so? The ozone layer, which filters out the dangerous ultraviolet light, has been thinning. For every one percent change in the ozone layer there can be a six percent increase in the number of skin cancers in both young and older people.

The best remedy is prevention. You cannot undo past overexposure to the sun. But you can do something to prevent further damage. Whenever you go out in the sun be sure to apply a sun block with a sun-protection factor (SPF) of at least 15—not just in the summer sun, but in the winter sun as well. Sun reflected off snow is just as damaging as summer sun, if not more so.

Tanning booths can be detrimental to the skin too. Even though tanning booths and beds emit ultraviolet A (UVA) radiation, which is supposedly safer than ultraviolet B (UVB) radiation from the sun, it can still pose hazards.

While UVA radiation does not cause an immediate sunburn (unless your skin is extremely sun-sensitive), continual use of tanning booths can cause effects on the skin similar to tanning outdoors.

Prevention of Skin Damage from the Sun

The best way to protect the skin against the long-term effects of sun abuse is to spend less time attempting to get a tan and to realize that a light tan—a healthy glow—is a lot more attractive than a deep, dark tan. In fact, a dark tan tends to make a woman look six to ten years older!

Years ago a dark tan was considered beautiful. These days people are beginning to realize that beauty is hidden rather than enhanced by dark tanning. In addition, even if beauty were enhanced by a dark tan, think of how foolish it is to sacrifice the future for a short-lived tan that fades in a matter of weeks.

The next thing to do is to be sure to apply plenty of sun block with an SPF of 15 and above. Be sure to apply the sun block twenty to thirty minutes before going out into the sun. It takes that long for the skin to absorb and use the lotion. If you do not allow that time you will burn for the first twenty to thirty minutes. This is the most common mistake people make, and they never know why they burned. Often, they blame it on the particular brand of sunblock they happened to use that day.

Your Posture Adds to Your Beauty

Good posture involves strong, healthy muscles. If you follow the workout we prescribe, you'll find that you sit, stand, and walk with greater ease, because your antigravity muscles will be working for you rather than against you. You'll also find that you're not as tired and not as tempted to slouch.

Perhaps you've fallen into bad habits, and you notice that your posture is especially poor. For example, if you notice that you tend to walk with your head thrust forward, or if you have rounded shoulders or swayback, here are some simple postural exercises that can be done every morning.

Head Thrust Forward

Lie flat on your back on a flat surface (the floor or a bench), and press your head into the floor or bench for five seconds. (Try to get your neck to rest flat on the floor.) Relax for five seconds and repeat. Do five sets of this movement.

Rounded Shoulders

Lie flat on your back on a flat exercise bench with a three-pound dumbbell in each hand. Extend your arms straight out at your sides, in line with your chest. Without straining, lower the dumbbells as far as you can go, gradually letting them sink lower and lower. At the lowest position, hold for five seconds, then relax. Repeat the movement five times.

Swayback

Lie flat on your back on the floor or on a flat exercise bench. Bend your knees slightly. Flex your abdominal muscles as hard as possible, and at the same time press your lower back into the floor by rotating your pelvis backward. Try to touch the floor or bench with your lower back. Hold the position for five seconds, then relax. Repeat the movement five times.

Take Care of Your Feet

There are twenty-six bones in the foot. When you wear high-heeled or pointy-toed shoes, you put a great deal of pressure on those bones. In addition, you press the nerves and ligaments of the foot together. The end result can be pain as well as the deformity of your beautiful feet.

When you wear high-heeled shoes you decrease the walking surface of the foot. This puts undue pressure on the calf muscles and sometimes even the quadriceps muscles.

High heels do make the leg appear longer and more shapely. Most women, the authors included, would never give up our high heels. However, we do advise that you limit wearing them. Wear high heels no longer than five hours at a time—in the evening, and when you won't be doing that much walking. If you get the chance and no one will notice, slip them off for ten minutes here and there. Try to avoid walking around in high-heeled shoes all day if you can.

If you must wear high-heeled shoes for any length of time, be sure that you have enough space in the shoe to wiggle your toes, and also get a cushioned sole. Try not to wear heels higher than three inches. Be sure to give your feet a treat by wearing rubber-soled walking or running shoes the day after you wear high-heeled shoes all day.

Fortunately, the calf exercises in this book will help strengthen and heal any damage done to your leg by wearing high-heeled shoes.

Your toes may be damaged by corns, calluses, or bunions if your shoes are too tight. Corns and calluses (tough skin built up as a result of continual pressure on a specific area) should be removed by a qualified podiatrist. If you try to do it yourself with home removal kits or razor blades, chances are the corns will return and/or you will injure yourself.

If you develop bunions (swollen joints at the base of the big toe) from wearing high heels, consult your doctor as to whether surgery is in order. Chances are he'll advise you to wear roomier shoes and to limit wearing high heels.

We love to pamper ourselves and to feel beautiful. Many of us go to beauty salons and get facials. We go to health spas and get herbal wraps, and so on. But most of us forget that a foot massage is the most wonderful thing in the world. Treat yourself. Look in your local telephone directory under "Reflexology." You may find that it's one of the most important phone calls you ever make.

There's Never a Vacation from Beauty or Fitness

Many women ask us, "What should we do when we go on vacation?" Our answer is: Everything in moderation. You can break good eating habits for a day or two, but not for a week or two. You can always find nutritious, low-fat, low-calorie foods on a menu. What restaurant doesn't have a baked potato, broiled fish, or chicken, a tossed salad, and steamed vegetables, for example? Clearly, the problem is not with the restaurant, but with our resolve.

There's also no reason to completely vegetate while on vacation. Aside from the walking you'll most likely do on your own, we suggest you do "The Twelve-Minute Total-Body Workout" every morning (see Bibliography). It will help keep your muscles tight and toned for weeks at a time while you're unable to do your regular workout.

And here's an idea. Instead of going to a place that's conducive to overeating, overindulgence in alcoholic beverages, and lying about in the sun all day, why not choose a health spa where you can enjoy healthful living for a week or two and learn how to improve various aspects of your life? There you can be pampered with massages, treatments, exercising, and eating right. Instead of coming home from your vacation feeling you need another one, you'll come home feeling refreshed. Think about it. It might be a good change!

Bibliography

Exercise Books for Additional Training

Kneuer, Cameo, and Joyce L. Vedral, Ph.D. *Cameo Fitness*. New York: Warner Books, 1990.

McLish, Rachel, and Joyce L. Vedral, Ph.D. *Perfect Parts*. New York: Warner Books, 1987.

Portugues, Gladys, and Joyce L. Vedral, Ph.D. *Hard Bodies*. New York: Dell Publishing, 1986.

Portugues, Gladys, and Joyce L. Vedral, Ph.D. *Hard Bodies Express Workout*. New York: Dell Publishing, 1988.

Vedral, Joyce, Ph.D. *Now or Never*. New York: Warner Books, 1986.

Vedral, Joyce, Ph.D. *The Fat-Burning Workout*. New York: Warner Books, 1991.

Vedral, Joyce, Ph.D. *The Twelve-Minute Total-Body Workout*. New York: Warner Books, 1989.

Vedral, Joyce, Ph.D. *Gut Busters*. New York: Warner Books, 1992.

Weider, Betty and Joe. *The Weider Body Book*. Chicago: Contemporary Books, 1984.

Weider, Betty and Joe. *The Weider Book of Bodybuilding for Women*. Chicago: Contemporary Books, 1981.

Weider, Joe. *Joe Weider's Ultimate Bodybuilding*. Chicago: Contemporary Books, 1989.

Weider, Joe, with Bill Reynolds. *The Weider System of Bodybuilding*. Chicago: Contemporary Books, 1983.

Nutrition Books

Burrows, Laurie Grad. *Make It Easy, Make It Light*. New York: Simon & Schuster, 1987.

Hausman, Patricia, M.S. *The Calcium Bible*. New York: Rawson Associates, 1985.

Katahn, Martin, Ph.D., and Jaimie Pope-Cordle, M.S., R.D. *Fat Gram Counter*. New York: W. W. Norton & Company, 1989.

Mindell, Earl. *Earl Mindell's New and Revised Vitamin Bible*. New York: Warner Books, 1985.

Natow, Annette B., Ph.D. *The Fat Attack Plan*. New York: Pocket Books, 1990.

Netzer, Corinne T. *The Corinne T. Netzer Encyclopedia of Food Values*. New York: Dell Publishing, 1992.

Reynolds, Bill, and Joyce L. Vedral. *Supercut: Nutrition for the Ultimate Physique*. Chicago: Contemporary Books, 1985.

Weider, Joe. *Nutrition and Training for Women Bodybuilders*. Chicago: Contemporary Books, 1984.

Magazines for Exercise and Nutritional Information

American Health, 28 West 23rd Street, New York, N.Y. 10010.
Longevity, 1965 Broadway, New York, N.Y. 10023-5965.
Muscle and Fitness, 21100 Erwin Street, Woodland Hills, Calif. 91367.
Shape, 21100 Erwin Street, Woodland Hills, Calif. 91367.
Your Health, 540 N.W. Broken Sound Blvd., Boca Raton, Fla. 33431.

Newsletters for Nutritional Information

"Mayo Clinic Nutrition Letter," 200 First Street, S.W., Rochester, Minn. 55905.
"Tufts University Diet and Nutrition Letter," P. O. Box 57857, Boulder, Colo. 80322-7857.
"University of California at Berkeley Wellness Letter," Health Letter Associates, P. O. Box 420148, Palm Coast, Fla. 32142.